REVOLUTION THROUGH PEACE

WORLD PERSPECTIVES

Volumes already published

WORLD PERSPECTIVES · *Volume Forty-five*

Planned and Edited by RUTH NANDA ANSHEN

REVOLUTION
THROUGH PEACE

by DOM HÉLDER CÂMARA

Translated from the Portuguese by Amparo McLean

1817

HARPER & ROW, PUBLISHERS

NEW YORK, EVANSTON, SAN FRANCISCO, LONDON

This book was formerly published in Brazil under the title *Revolução Dentro da Paz*.

About This Book

Friends of Dom Hélder Câmara have already distributed selected passages on certain themes from his writings, speeches, lectures, congratulatory prayers and sermons.

Dom Hélder held out as long as he could against the idea of seeing in a book words that he had thought destined at most to the ephemeral life of newspapers and magazines.

What finally persuaded him to publish these sermons was the thought that some books are depositions, declarations of faith.

The title is his: *Revolution Through Peace*

32222

Contents

World Perspectives

What This Series Means

It is the thesis of *World Perspectives* that man is in the process of developing a new consciousness which, in spite of his apparent spiritual and moral captivity, can eventually lift the human race above and beyond the fear, ignorance, and isolation which beset it today. It is to this nascent consciousness, to this concept of man born out of a universe perceived through a fresh vision of reality, that *World Perspectives* is dedicated.

My Introduction to this Series is not of course to be construed as a prefatory essay for each individual book. These few pages simply attempt to set forth the general aim and purpose of the Series as a whole. They try to point to the principle of permanence within change and to define the essential nature of man, as presented by those scholars who have been invited to participate in this intellectual and spiritual movement.

Man has entered a new era of evolutionary history, one in which rapid change is a dominant consequence. He is contending with a fundamental change, since he has intervened in the evolutionary process. He must now better appreciate this fact and then develop the wisdom to direct the process toward his fulfillment rather than toward his destruction. As he learns to apply his understanding of the physical world for practical purposes, he is, in reality, extending his innate capacity and augmenting his ability and his need to communicate as well as his ability to think and to create. And as a result, he is substituting a goal-directed evolutionary process in his struggle against environmental hardship for the slow, but effective, biological evolution which produced modern man through mutation and natural selection. By intelligent intervention in the evolutionary process man has greatly accelerated and greatly expanded the range of his possibilities. But he has not changed the basic fact that it remains a trial and error process, with the danger of taking paths that lead to sterility of mind and heart, moral apathy and intellectual inertia; and even producing social dinosaurs unfit to live in an evolving world.

Only those spiritual and intellectual leaders of our epoch who have a paternity in this extension of man's horizons are invited to participate in this Series: those who are aware of the truth that beyond the divisiveness among men there exists a primordial unitive power since we are all bound together by a common humanity more fundamental than any unity of dogma; those who recognize that the centrifugal force which has scattered and atomized mankind must be replaced by an integrating structure and process capable of bestowing meaning and purpose on existence; those who realize that science itself, when not inhibited by the limitations of its own methodology, when chastened and humbled, commits man to an indeterminate range of yet undreamed consequences that may flow from it.

Virtually all of our disciplines have relied on conceptions which are now incompatible with the Cartesian axiom, and with the static world view we once derived from it. For underlying the new ideas, including those of modern physics, is a unifying order, but it is not causality; it is purpose, and not the purpose of the universe and of man, but the purpose *in* the universe and *in* man. In other words, we seem to inhabit a world of dynamic process and structure. Therefore we need a calculus of potentiality rather than one of probability, a dialectic of polarity, one in which unity and diversity are redefined as simultaneous and necessary poles of the same essence.

Our situation is new. No civilization has previously had to face the challenge of scientific specialization, and our response must be new. Thus this Series is committed to ensure that the spiritual and moral needs of man as a human being and the scientific and intellectual resources at his command for *life* may be brought into a productive, meaningful and creative harmony.

In a certain sense we may say that man now has regained his former geocentric position in the universe. For a picture of the Earth has been made available from distant space, from the lunar desert, and the sheer isolation of the Earth has become plain. This is as new and as powerful an idea in history as any that has ever been born in man's consciousness. We are all becoming seriously concerned with our natural environment. And this concern is not only the result of the warnings given by biologists, ecologists and conservationists. Rather it is the result of a deepening awareness that something new has happened, that the planet Earth is a unique and precious place. Indeed, it may not be a mere coincidence that this awareness should have been born at the exact moment when man took his first step into outer space.

This Series endeavors to point to a reality of which scientific theory has revealed only one aspect. It is the commitment to this reality that lends universal intent to a scientist's most original and solitary thought. By acknowledging this frankly we shall restore science to the great family of human aspirations by which men hope to fulfill themselves in the world community as thinking and sentient beings. For our problem is to discover a principle of differentiation and yet relationship lucid enough to justify and to purify scientific, philosophic and all other knowledge, both discursive and intuitive, by accepting their interdependence. This is the crisis in consciousness made articulate through the crisis in science. This is the new awakening.

Each volume presents the thought and belief of its author and points to the way in which religion, philosophy, art, science, economics, politics and history may constitute that form of human activity which takes the fullest and most precise account of variousness, possibility, complexity and difficulty. Thus *World Perspectives* endeavors to define that ecumenical power of the mind and heart which enables man through his mysterious greatness to re-create his life.

This Series is committed to a re-examination of all those sides of human endeavor which the specialist was taught to believe he could safely leave aside. It attempts to show the structural kinship between subject and object; the indwelling of the one in the other. It interprets present and past events impinging on human life in our growing World Age and envisages what man may yet attain when summoned by an unbending inner necessity to the quest of what is most exalted in him. Its purpose is to offer new vistas in terms of world and human development while refusing to betray the intimate correlation between universality and individuality, dynamics and form, freedom and destiny. Each author deals with the increasing realization that spirit and nature are not separate and apart; that intuition and reason must regain their importance as the means of perceiving and fusing inner being with outer reality.

World Perspectives endeavors to show that the conception of wholeness, unity, organism is a higher and more concrete conception than that of matter and energy. Thus an enlarged meaning of life, of biology, not as it is revealed in the test tube of the laboratory but as it is experienced within the organism of life itself, is attempted in this Series. For the principle of life consists in the tension which connects spirit with the realm of matter, symbiotically joined. The element of life is dominant in the very texture of nature, thus rendering life, biology, a trans-empirical science. The laws of life have their origin beyond their mere physical manifestations and compel us to consider their spiritual source. In fact, the widening of the conceptual framework has not only served to restore order within the respective branches of knowledge, but has also disclosed analogies in man's position regarding the analysis and synthesis of experience in apparently separated domains of knowledge, suggesting the possibility of an ever more embracing objective description of the meaning of life.

Knowledge, it is shown in these books, no longer consists in a manipulation of man and nature as opposite forces, nor in the reduction of data to mere statistical order, but is a means of liberating mankind from the destructive power of fear, pointing the way toward the goal of the rehabilitation of the human will and the rebirth of faith and confidence in the human person. The works published also endeavor to reveal that the cry for patterns, systems and authorities is growing less insistent as the desire grows stronger in both East and West for the recovery of a dignity, integrity and self-realization which are the inalienable rights of man who may now guide change by means of conscious purpose in the light of rational experience.

The volumes in this Series endeavor to demonstrate that only in a society in which awareness of the problems of science exists, can its discoveries start great waves of change in human culture, and in such a manner that these discoveries may deepen and not erode the sense of universal human community. The differences in the disciplines, their epistemological exclusiveness, the variety of historical experiences, the differences of traditions, of cultures, of languages, of the arts, should be protected and preserved. But the interrelationship and unity of the whole should at the same time be accepted.

The authors of *World Perspectives* are of course aware that the ultimate answers to the hopes and fears which pervade modern society rest on the moral fibre of man, and on the wisdom and responsibility of those who promote the course of its development. But moral decisions cannot dispense with an insight into the interplay of the objective elements which offer and limit the choices made. Therefore an understanding of what the issues are, though not a sufficient condition, is a necessary prerequisite for directing action toward constructive solutions.

Other vital questions explored relate to problems of international understanding as well as to problems dealing with prejudice and the resultant tensions and antagonisms. The growing perception and responsibility of our World Age point to the new reality that the individual person and the collective person supplement and integrate each other; that the thrall of totalitarianism of both left and right has been shaken in the universal desire to recapture the authority of truth and human totality. Mankind can finally place its trust not in a proletarian authoritarianism, not in a secularized humanism, both of which have betrayed the spiritual property right of history, but in a sacramental brotherhood and in the unity of knowledge. This new consciousness has created a widening of human horizons beyond every parochialism, and a revolution in human thought comparable to the basic assumption, among the ancient Greeks, of the sovereignty of reason; corresponding to the great effulgence of the moral conscience articulated by the Hebrew prophets; analogous to the fundamental assertions of Christianity; or to the beginning of the new scientific era, the era of the science of dynamics, the experimental foundations of which were laid by Galileo in the Renaissance.

An important effort of this Series is to re-examine the contradictory meanings and applications which are given today to such terms as democracy, freedom, justice, love, peace, brotherhood and God. The purpose of such inquiries is to clear the way for the foundation of a genuine *world* history not in terms of nation or race or culture but in terms of man in relation to God, to himself, his fellow man and the universe, that reach beyond immediate self-interest. For the meaning of the World Age consists in respecting man's hopes and dreams which lead to a deeper understanding of the basic values of all peoples.

World Perspectives is planned to gain insight into the meaning of man, who not only is determined by history but who also determines history. History is to be understood as concerned not only with the life of man on this planet but as including also such cosmic influences as interpenetrate our human world. This generation is discovering that history does not conform to the social optimism of modern civilization and that the organization of human communities and the establishment of freedom and peace are not only intellectual achievements but spiritual and moral achievements as well, demanding a cherishing of the wholeness of human personality, the "unmediated wholeness of feeling and thought," and constituting a never-ending challenge to man, emerging from the abyss of meaninglessness and suffering, to be renewed and replenished in the totality of his life.

Justice itself, which has been "in a state of pilgrimage and crucifixion" and now is being slowly liberated from the grip of social and political demonologies in the East as well as in the West, begins to question its own premises. The modern revolutionary movements which have challenged the sacred institutions of society by protecting social injustice in the name of social justice are here examined and re-evaluated.

In the light of this, we have no choice but to admit that the *un*freedom against which freedom is measured must be retained with it, namely, that the aspect of truth out of which the night view appears to emerge, the darkness of our time, is as little abandonable as is man's subjective advance. Thus the two sources of man's consciousness are inseparable, not as dead but as living and complementary, an aspect of that "principle of complementarity" through which Niels Bohr has sought to unite the quantum and the wave, both of which constitute the very fabric of life's radiant energy.

There is in mankind today a counterforce to the sterility and danger of a quantitative, anonymous mass culture; a new, if sometimes imperceptible, spiritual sense of convergence toward human and world unity on the basis of the sacredness of each human person and respect for the plurality of cultures. There is a growing awareness that equality may not be evaluated in mere numerical terms but is proportionate and analogical in its reality. For when equality is equated with interchangeability, individuality is negated and the human person transmuted into a faceless mask.

We stand at the brink of an age of a world in which human life presses forward to actualize new forms. The false separation of man and nature, of time and space, of freedom and security, is acknowledged, and we are faced with a new vision of man in his organic unity and of history offering a richness and diversity of quality and majesty of scope hitherto unprecedented. In relating the accumulated wisdom of man's spirit to the new reality of the World Age, in articulating its thought and belief, *World Perspectives* seeks to encourage a renaissance of hope in society and of pride in man's decision as to what his destiny will be.

World Perspectives is committed to the recognition that all great changes are preceded by a vigorous intellectual re-evaluation and reorganization. Our authors are aware that the sin of *hubris* may be avoided by showing that the creative process itself is not a free activity if by free we mean arbitrary, or unrelated to cosmic law. For the creative process in the human mind, the developmental process in organic nature and the basic laws of the inorganic realm may be but varied expressions of a universal formative process. Thus *World Perspectives* hopes to show that although the present apocalyptic period is one of exceptional tensions, there is also at work an exceptional movement toward a compensating unity which refuses to violate the ultimate moral power at work in the universe, that very power upon which all human effort must at last depend. In this way we may come to understand that there exists an inherent independence of spiritual and mental growth which, though conditioned by circumstances, is never determined by circumstances. In this way the great plethora of human knowledge may be correlated with an insight into the nature of human nature by being attuned to the wide and deep range of human thought and human experience.

Incoherence is the result of the present disintegrative processes in education. Thus the need for *World Perspectives* expresses itself in the recognition that natural and man-made ecological systems require as much study as isolated particles and elementary reactions. For there is a basic correlation of elements in nature as in man which cannot be separated, which compose each other and alter each other mutually. Thus we hope to widen appropriately our conceptual framework of reference. For our epistemological problem consists in our finding the proper balance between our lack of an all-embracing principle relevant to our way of evaluating life and in our power to express ourselves in a logically consistent manner.

Our Judeo-Christian and Greco-Roman heritage, our Hellenic tradition, has compelled us to think in exclusive categories. But our *experience* challenges us to recognize a totality richer and far more complex than the average observer could have suspected—a totality which compels him to think in ways which the logic of dichotomies denies. We are summoned to revise fundamentally our ordinary ways of conceiving experience, and thus, by expanding our vision and by accepting those forms of thought which also include nonexclusive categories, the mind is then able to grasp what it was incapable of grasping or accepting before.

In spite of the infinite obligation of men and in spite of their finite power, in spite of the intransigence of nationalisms, and in spite of the homelessness of moral passions rendered ineffectual by the technological outlook, beneath the apparent turmoil and upheaval of the present, and out of the transformations of this dynamic period with the unfolding of a world-consciousness, the purpose of *World Perspectives* is to help quicken the "unshaken heart of well-rounded truth" and interpret the significant elements of the World Age now taking shape out of the core of that undimmed continuity of the creative process which restores man to mankind while deepening and enhancing his communion with the universe.

RUTH NANDA ANSHEN

REVOLUTION THROUGH PEACE

1

Evangelism and Humanism

Our beloved Dom Carlos Coelho has unexpectedly been taken from us, and Providence has taken me by the hand and led me back to Olinda and Recife. Pope Paul VI, with his deep knowledge of conditions in Latin America and Brazil, decided that this key post in the Brazilian Northeast should be filled with no loss of time, and my inauguration was scheduled, therefore, for the Sunday of the Good Shepherd.

I pray that we be given Grace to read rightly the signs of the times, to keep up with events, to fall in with God's plans. Together, let us try to understand what is happening. Let us talk a little about the spirit that moves me as I begin my pastoral mission. Let us talk for a moment about our initial plans and suggestions.

When Dom Sebastião Leme came here, as I do, from Rio de Janeiro in 1916, he wrote a pastoral letter which became a classic as soon as it was written. What would the great Dom Leme have to say about the Brazilian Northeast in 1964? What does our beloved Dom Carlos whisper from Heaven? How will the Holy Ghost which brought me here inspire me?

Who am I and to whom am I speaking, or rather, to whom do I wish to speak? I am a man of the Northeast, talking to other *nordestinos,* with his eyes on Brazil, on Latin America, and on the rest of the world. A human being who considers himself a brother in frailty and sin of men of all races and all corners of the world. A Christian addressing Christians, with his heart ecumenically open to men of all creeds and ideologies. A Catho-

1

lic bishop who, imitating Christ, has come not to be served but
to serve.

Catholics and non-Catholics, believers and nonbelievers,
hear my fraternal greeting: Our Lord Jesus Christ be praised.

The bishop belongs to everyone. Let none be scandalized
when they see me in the company of individuals considered unworthy and sinful. Which of us is not a sinner? Who will cast
the first stone? Our Lord, when accused of walking with publi-
cans and eating with sinners, replied that it is the sick man
who needs a physician.

Let none be amazed if they see me with individuals considered
insidious and dangerous, leftists or rightists, in power or out,
anti-reformist or reformist, anti-revolutionary or revolutionary,
men of good faith and bad.

Let none try to confine me to one group or link me to any
one party, insist that his friends be my friends and his enemies
mine.

My door and my heart will be open to everyone, without
any exception whatever. Christ died for all men: it is not for
me to exclude anyone from this fraternal dialogue.

Have I come to look after the poor? Of course I have, since
loving all men, I am bound to follow Christ's example and
have a special love for the poor. At the last judgment we shall
all be judged according to the treatment we have given Christ,
Christ in the person of those who are hungry, thirsty, dirty,
sick, and oppressed. . . .

We will carry on the normal activities of this archdiocese
and care for the poor, seeking out in particular the poverty
which hides its head in shame. We will endeavor to keep poverty
from sinking into misery. Poverty can and at times should be a
gift received in a generous spirit or given as a spontaneous offering to our Father. Misery, on the other hand, is revolting and
degrading: it mars the image of God revealed in every man;
it violates the right and duty of every human being to seek
wholeness and perfection.

Naturally the *mocambos* and the abandoned children are

uppermost in our thoughts. Whoever is suffering, whether in body or soul; whoever is in despair, be he poor or rich, will have a special place in the heart of the Bishop. But I have not come here to help anyone delude himself into thinking that a little charity and social work will suffice. There is no doubt about it: there is crying misery to which we have no right to remain indifferent. Very often, we have no choice but to take immediate action, however inadequate. But let us not deceive ourselves into thinking that the problem is limited to a few gestures of reform; let us not confuse the beautiful and indispensable idea of order, the end of all human progress, with the mockery of order which is responsible for preserving structures we all know should not and cannot be preserved.

If we really want to get to the root of our social ills, we will have to help our country break out of the vicious circle of underdevelopment and misery. There are those who are shocked to hear anyone say that this is our number one social problem. There are those who think it demagoguery when anyone calls their attention to human beings living in conditions that can only be described as inhuman.

Once the bishops of the Northeast asked government technicians to join forces with them in an effort to pool the meager funds and scarce specialists who were being wasted on ineffective, scattered efforts. This pioneering attitude contributed to the creation of SUDENE, the Superintendency for the Development of the Northeast, which we hope will always merit our support as an instrument designed to break down the criminal imbalance between the highly progressive areas of our country and those that are stagnating in misery. SUDENE is making it possible for foreign capital to contribute, on terms that are perfectly compatible with national dignity; but what is even more welcome, the South is beginning to invest in the Northeast.

But development does not trickle down from the top; it cannot be imposed from above. Let us not be afraid of valid ideas, however much they may have been bandied about: development implies an awakening of social consciousness, of civic responsibility, of culture, self-awareness, and technical planning.

The Church cannot stand apart from history. Through her free, adult, responsible laymen, she lives at its very heart.

Christ specifically entrusted the mission of spreading the Gospel to the hierarchy of the Church. But in no circumstances did He wish to keep the Christian community apart from the great adventure of human development. On the contrary, it is up to the Christian layman to shoulder his responsibilities on the front line. We have great faith in those Christians who are committed to what is real and bear witness of it to Christ. We must begin our technical planning without delay, in all the complexity which that implies. If the risk of creating an elite technocracy is to be avoided, it is necessary for the whole Northeastern community to be alert and responsible and to assume the burden of planning the region's development. It is imperative that we help form cadres of experts at all levels. We can serenely trust the people of the Northeast to work out their own development from the soil and climate God has given us. Let us help make the Northeast a developing community, open to Brazil and to the world.

For any of you who may be astonished at the tenor of this message, who may be troubled at the Bishop's ideas or his language, let me explain my reasoning. God made us in such a way that our intelligence turns always toward the truth. When we cling to error, it is because our minds have been seduced by the kernel of truth that exists in every error. The best way of combating error is to free the kernels of truth imprisoned within it, for when error is deprived of the truth concealed in it, it loses its inner consistency and its power to tempt us.

Let us have enough serenity of mind and Christian courage to rescue the good ideas clothed in expressions which just now have the sound of ugly, forbidden words. Popular culture; *conscientização;** politization; self-awareness—perhaps these

* *Conscientização:* The awakening of social consciousness. The term was popularized in the early 1960's by Paulo Freire (now in exile) and other educators

labels should be temporarily forgotten or even changed. But we should not cast down banners of truth for the sole reason that they were once carried in the wrong hands. Why should we be afraid of movements which can only be of interest in a genuine democracy and cannot be carried out except by regimes with a respect for liberty? Why should we be afraid of movements which are profoundly and essentially Christian?

It would be an unpardonable scandal if the Church were to abandon the masses in their hour of greatest need, as if she took no interest in helping them reach a level of human, Christian dignity compatible with real citizenship.

All of us here believe that all men are children of the same Father in heaven. Men who have the same father are brothers. Let us treat one another like brothers!

All of us believe that God made man in His own image and likeness and commanded him to master nature and finish the work of Creation. Let us do the possible and the impossible to ensure that every job in the Northeast is one capable of making the man who does it feel he is helping the Creator build the world!

All of us believe that freedom is a divine gift to be preserved at all costs. In the highest and deepest sense of the word, let us liberate all of the human creatures who dwell among us.

All of us believe that the ideal to strive for is the development of the whole man and of all men. In our time we see before our eyes examples of religious indifference and even atheism beginning to spread in the highly developed countries. But the end of development is not to forget our God. The more we advance in material progress, the more we need a strong, enlightened faith to illuminate the building of a new Northeast from within.

At the moment all of this is vague. But we are going to live together, *we are going to live together,* by the grace of God. And

who conducted adult literacy campaigns in the Northeast and elsewhere, designed to make the pupil emotionally, intellectually, and politically aware of himself and his surroundings.

so we will examine together every one of these affirmations, from every point of view. We will study them carefully and find ways to make them come true. This does not mean— and I cannot repeat this too often—that the Church will be committed to any one person, party, or movement, whether political or economic.

The Church has no desire to steer the course of events. She wants to serve men by helping to make them free. And she will be at hand to say that this liberation, which *begins in time,* will not be consummated until the Son of God returns at the end of time, in that Second Coming which will be the true beginning.

Do you remember the awesome spectacle of Pope John's death? It seems to me that one great lesson stands out among all the lessons to be learned from that unforgettable scene: when Catholics and non-Catholics, believers and nonbelievers —men of all races, creeds, and ideologies—followed the Pope's death agony with distress and wept over his death as if they were mourning the loss of a father, what the people were saying implicitly was that every priest, every bishop, ought to be as good as Pope John.

As for the Good Shepherd, He transcends the centuries, but in every age He takes the form called for by the times. Keep this final image in your hearts: do you know what sheep it is that Christ bears on His shoulders as He walks today's roads? All you have to do is open your eyes and look around you: the Good Shepherd is carrying on His shoulders the underdeveloped world.

Here as everywhere else in the world, seminaries are institutions whose aim it is to prepare priests; and here as in every other corner of the earth, the priest's essential mission is to proclaim the good tidings of Salvation. But the Church as Christ's follower has a clear sense of reality: she knows how to discover the tasks she is specifically called upon to carry out, here and now, in the circumstances of time and place in which she finds herself. For anyone with eyes to see, now, just as the decade of development is beginning, a new seminary in Recife is opening to the heart of the Brazilian Northeast.

So far, as it happens, the essential meaning of the great and beautiful idea of development has been truncated and many of its implications sacrificed. The idea of economic development has been complemented only by that of social development. At most, one region's development has been taken as a starting point for the development of a whole country.

The Regional Seminary of Recife has been born with the mission of giving human breadth and significance to the idea of development, and to add that new dimension which the supernatural brings to the limits of human thought.

The Regional Seminary, faithful to its mission of service and trusting in God, Who makes use of humble instruments, was born attentive to a circumstance it considers providential: Latin America occupies a singular position in the confrontation between the developed and the developing worlds. It so happens that in Latin America it is Brazil, in Brazil the Northeast, in the Northeast Recife—and who knows, in Recife perhaps the Regional Seminary—which has a mission to fulfill, a duty to perform.

To understand this question is to understand how right Rome was to virtually demand that this seminary be established. It was a sure and discreet way to take part in the development process, the most universal, important, and urgent problem facing humanity in our time.

This House will educate priests to evangelize. But one does not evangelize abstract, intemporal beings suspended in air. One evangelizes human beings of flesh and blood, introduced into space and time.

We bishops of the Northeast found we had no choice but to encourage the farm workers to organize into unions as the only practicable way to enable them to discuss their rights with landowners who more often than not were transplanted straight from the Middle Ages into this twenty-first century in which mankind has already begun to live.

Did we exceed our mission or forget that we are the heralds of the mystery of true salvation? By no means. We know that in temporal matters it is incumbent upon us as bishops to throw the light of theology on the actions of laymen. And here is where laymen have a specific mission that cannot be evaded. We know it is up to us to encourage technicians whose good faith and competence we are bound to respect. (And why not pause for a moment to salute the *développeurs,* the noble and responsible features of whose task have been analyzed so well by that master in the art of development, Father Lebret?)

It is far from our intention to stop at economic development; we begin there because our Father has not endowed us purely with spirit. And if we feel obliged to help rather than simply to leave to laymen the work which would normally be a sign of Christian presence in the temporal world, it is because we feel compelled to do so, faced as we are with the blindness, the coldheartedness, and the arrogance of certain lords of the world. We feel the necessity to lend our moral support to the fundamental task of defending human rights. If even bishops of the Holy Church, who have been entrusted with the most Christian mission of defending downtrodden human beings, are with impunity branded as Communists, what would happen to our priests, and above all to our laymen, if we abandoned them to their fate?

Though we almost always begin with the practical necessity of fostering economic development, our religious convictions and our love for our fellow creatures lead us far beyond the economic or even the purely social realm. Our watchword for development is the word of Christ:

I came that they may have life, and have it more abundantly.

We will not rest until the Northeast passes from its present state of underdevelopment to the abundant life which can only be a reality when Divine Grace fills and transcends man's limitations and makes us participants in the nature of God.

It is exciting to work in the Northeast. When we say the region is still underdeveloped, we must forget that in 1964, when the gross national product of Brazil slid back 3 percent, that of the Northeast increased by 6 percent, thanks to the application of regional solutions. This proves the region's capacity. When we declare that we want to bring the Northeast to full development, this implies the crowning glory of spiritual development; it does not mean that we are forgetting the beautiful religious impulse of which the Recife Seminary is a sign.

The Church is present in the world. The Church is present in the building of the world. The Church is present in man's effort to humanize the world. No one should be startled at the expression "humanize"; if man is linked to God through the Man-God, humanizing the world means cleansing Creation of every mark of sin, so that man may attain his fullest measure of development.

You therefore are to be perfect, even as your heavenly Father is perfect.

Which is more difficult and more exciting: to humanize subhuman men made wretched by misery, or to humanize supermen dehumanized by luxury? The two tasks complement each other in such a way that the realization of each is dependent on that of the other.

It is time for God's people in the underdeveloped world to throw themselves heart and soul into the struggle to develop the sons of God who have been reduced to subhuman dimensions by a subhuman life. The Latin-American bishops who met in Mar del Plata decided there that the Church must assume an active role in the development and integration of the Latin-American continent.

In this century of the European Common Market and other great economic empires which would like to divide the world among themselves, the scale of production must be continental. It is in no way our wish to encourage the world to divide itself into gigantic and selfish continental groupings. But experience has taught us that genuine dialogue between the very strong and the very weak is impossible. (The people say, in their clear and picturesque language, that a sardine and a shark can't be friends.)

We must draw the necessary conclusions from the precious teaching that "development is the new name for peace." Anyone who accepts this lesson of Feltin, given immortality when it was adopted by the Pope, must know that keeping 80 percent of humanity in a state of underdevelopment and hunger can only lead to the most terrible of wars. We must not commit a sin of omission. We cannot remain outside the struggle. We have a human and Christian duty to take part in it.

It may seem futile to think of a unified Asia or a unified Africa, when Asia and Africa lack many of the elements of integration which Latin America is fortunate enough to possess. Here we speak sister languages and our only religion, for all practical purposes, is Christianity. In Africa there are more than one thousand languages, and as for Asia, India alone has over two hundred. On the matter of religion, we know the Afro-Asian world has many, from Buddhism to Islam, from Shintoism to Hinduism, from Christianity to animism. And yet, in spite of that enormous diversity of race, language, and religion, Africa and Asia astonished the white-skinned world by proclaiming at Bandung that only a union going beyond insignificant divisions and local interests would help the colored peoples emerge from their underdeveloped state to find a place in the sun.

If Africa and Asia wish to join Latin America in *UNCTAD*, and if Latin America wishes to go forward with Asia and Africa, let us do so effectually: we must take our part in the development and economic integration of the entire Third World. It would be a pity if peoples were drawn together solely by economic interest and the necessity to survive; a pity if religion were to be excluded, "alienated and alienating." If religion has no role at just those moments which these peoples see as decisive and in efforts which seem sacred to them, we will lose an exceptional opportunity of being useful and will be deprived of the necessary moral ascendancy to enable us to keep today's peaceful effort from being tomorrow's violent struggle, to keep the obstacles along the way from leading to hatred, and, above all, to see that the hard-won development to human status for yesterday's subhumans does not become a source of dehumanization tomorrow. . . .

Perhaps it would be a good thing if the Latin-American Episcopal Council were to make a filial suggestion to the Holy See that its Commission for Latin America be expanded into a Commission for the Third World, with the added responsibility of watching over "the right to social justice" and "the duty of universal charity" for the underdeveloped world.

By the same token, it would seem imperative that the bishops of the developed world meet to study ways of encouraging churchmen in a mighty effort to humanize the supermen who are being dehumanized by comfortable living. Is a harmonious fraternal civilization an impossible dream? Is it absurd to dream of world solidarity?

What is most distressing in the case of rural areas, where it is extremely urgent that the archaic structures still prevailing in so many countries be reformed, is that often admirable laws already exist, along with the complex bureaucracy needed to administer them. And yet years pass and the laws remain on paper, unenforced.

Meanwhile many people, especially young people and often the best of them, lose faith in democracy and turn to violence.

Who among us does not know, does not feel, that the time has come—that it came long since—to *carry out* agrarian reform instead of merely using it as a slogan and as the object of interminable studies and discussions? It is urgent, most urgent, to remember that the Christian Message is meant not only to be heard and admired, but to be lived.

Why do the bishops of Latin America, together with their priests and laymen, not rise from one end of this continent to the other and try to put the conclusions reached at Mar del Plata into practice?

A few isolated laymen, a few enthusiastic priests, a few bishops known as progressive would be vulnerable: it would be all too easy to denounce them as subversives and Communists.

But if all of God's people on this continent take a really active part in the development and integration of the Latin-American countries—and carry with them the universities, the technicians working for official government bureaus or private companies, leaders of every religion, business leaders, labor leaders, the written and spoken media, theater and the movies, every vital impulse of this continent—then perhaps we can act in time to keep Latin America from opting for violence, with all its unforeseeable consequences. Perhaps we can forestall in Latin America the explosion of the worst bomb of all, far more terrible than the A bomb or the H bomb: the M bomb, the Misery bomb.

Needless to say, it cannot be done in overtimid, overcautious little steps taken in slow motion. There is no engaging the enthusiasm of a continent without daring and greatness.

Do we not owe this witness, this example, this incentive to Africa and Asia, our sisters in underdevelopment? Does not the fact that we are the Christian continent, in name at least, lay special obligations upon us?

2

Science and Faith

The world would indeed be absurd if there were no Creator, no Father, as the Prime Mover at the beginning of beginnings, at the origin of all things. Grave misunderstandings have arisen in the past between theologians and men of science. The former felt obliged to interpret the Biblical account of Creation as if the Bible were intended to be a scientific treatise. It is hard for some people to understand that the all-important thing to be emphasized—yesterday, today, and forever—is the eternal presence of the Father-Creator. All the rest is only a way of making the story comprehensible to everyone. In a way, the Bible is the illustrious precursor of elaborate theatrical spectacles and comic books alike.

Some apologists have clung tenaciously to positions they believed to be the official doctrine of the Church, only to be forced to yield ground, step by step, when the evidence made clear the sheer stubborn fancy of maintaining such untenable positions. They were willing to admit, for example, that the days of Genesis were not twenty-four hours long, but were alarmed to see the supposed six thousand years since the Creation of the World stretching into millions. They were alarmed, too, at the idea of evolution, even though the evolution in question was not born of matter, or chaos, or the unknown, or fate, but of the Father-Creator.

Anyone who immersed himself in science was able to perceive that the accumulation of data from many different sources and viewpoints clearly proved evolution to be more than a mere scientific hypothesis, and it became increasingly difficult for such a person to accept the petty little God, so lacking in creative imagination, that was held up before him by pseudo-Christians.

Now that we are confident enough to accept the fact that the Creator may have deliberately chosen an evolutionary path to Creation, now that we have no difficulty in accepting whatever scientific measurements of time may be necessary, the dialogue between science and faith becomes easier every day.

Agnostics and atheists are disarmed when they see that we do not hesitate to admit that from the moment when man appeared on the scene, his Creator and Father, Who made him in His own image, Who made him His steward, entrusting to him the task of conquering nature and completing the work of Creation, also gave him the responsibility, and the glory, of carrying on evolution.

Instead of finishing the world down to the last detail and leaving man with nothing creative to do; instead of halfheartedly trusting him and leaving only the finishing touches to be made by His collaborator, God gave wide-ranging powers to man. We have only to think of the latest scientific discoveries, which are no doubt harbingers of numberless others, each more staggering to the imagination than the last. Now that he has split the atom and is preparing to make forays into space, now that he is only a hand's breadth away from the mastery of life itself, are there any bounds to man's destiny?

It is easy to understand the temptation to which man sometimes yields when the shadow of sin clouds his vision and inflames his egotism. Not content with the honor of being God's steward, he feels so strong and so powerful that he is mad enough to think he can manage very well without God. The fragile giant fails to perceive that his own discoveries are clouding his brain. Now that nuclear energy is in his hands, he can either provide every human being with a really human standard of living or eliminate all life from the face of the earth. With his power to raise to a human level millions and millions of fellow children of God whom stark misery has reduced to a subhuman existence, the superman does not even realize that excessive affluence and self-centeredness are reducing him, too, to a subhuman level.

Far from losing patience with man, Our Father sent His Divine Son to earth. Measuring man's thirst to become God, and knowing that, for all his greatness, man was doomed to remain at an infinite distance from the source of Divine Life, the Son of God became man incarnate, Man-God, so that man's dream of being God might be fulfilled.

That is why the never-ending struggle for development is a sacred battle. We must go beyond partial, unilateral development to help those who are something less than whole human beings, whether dehumanized by want or by their own selfishness, to live in the light of the boundless development, the infinite plenitude, of Divine Life itself.

Then and only then will development take on its full meaning: that of knowing more, producing more, having more in order to be more. And when we speak of Christ in the Mass— especially now that all can meaningfully participate in a Mass spoken in the vernacular—we are speaking also of ourselves, who became one with Him on the day of our baptism.

"For through Jesus Christ Our Lord, You unceasingly create these good things and sanctify them and give them life, You bless them and bestow them on us for our use."

This doctrine is eternal. It was not improvised hastily by a Church held at bay by science, with nowhere to turn. It has come down to us unchanged from the Holy Scriptures and the writings of the Church Fathers. But we of the Church must recognize that we left it dormant through centuries of winter, and if we have the joy of seeing it blossom forth in strength and beauty now, it is because we have been given the Grace of living in the springtime Pope John foretold when he announced the Ecumenical Council, Vatican II.

Now, after Vatican II, a scientist can feel at ease when taking part in a dialogue with the Church; he can understand how an engineer in the developing Northeast, even if he has no faith, may feel himself caught up in the active work that our Church is encouraging and trying to augment.

There is no way of getting around it: we must have the honesty to admit that the Catholic Church once gave exaggerated emphasis to dogmas which tended to leave Christians stranded by the side of the road to progress, which today we call development. We have sometimes exaggerated the conflict between matter and spirit, body and soul, almost crystallizing into dogma a conviction that the spirit was created by God but the body came close to being the work of the Devil.

On the other hand, when Christians looked at the world they were sometimes virtually induced to hate it, or at least to flee from it, since of all the various meanings of the expression "world" found in the Scriptures, only one was commonly singled out: that of the world as synonymous with sin. The passage in which Christ declares that He will not pray for the world was cited again and again.

If the Church continued to plow this deeply hollowed furrow, to drift with this negative current, how could she avoid the accusation of those who called her obscurantist, a roadblock in the way of progress? The program of Christian life would for all practical purposes be reduced to getting through the treacherous world as quickly as possible, never clinging to its trappings, thoughts firmly fixed on eternity.

Luckily there have also been theologians like the great Père Chenu to remind us that the Ecumenical Council, Vatican II, definitely established as authentic Church doctrine that:

- The body, too, was created by God and is the tabernacle of the Holy Trinity.
- Flesh can no longer be thought of as synonymous with sin, for the Word was made flesh and dwelt among us.
- If Christ truly warned that He would not pray for the world,

Scripture also tells us that God so loved the world that He sent His only begotten Son to save it.

People whose only contact with the Church has been through Christians who, though sincere, upright, and well intentioned, distort the Christian view of life by exaggerating certain aspects of the truth as though they were the whole of it, are amazed to see the Council give its wholehearted support to the theology of the here and now. They receive an impression of such swift and radical change that they may be pardoned for thinking that the Church, defeated by science and seeing no alternative, has been so Machiavellian as to pretend to embrace what it can no longer in conscience refuse to accept.

This is not the case at all. The Council did not invent on the spur of the moment the numerous texts on which it takes its stand. Those texts have always been there; they were merely overshadowed by others. It is our duty as Christians to study and become familiar with them, emphasize them, make them a part of our lives—and I am thinking especially of Christians in underdeveloped areas, whom the Holy Father has asked to play an active role in the effort of development. All of us must realize sooner or later that when man conquers nature and completes the work of Creation, he is following divine orders.

The euphoria which has overwhelmed man in recent years because he has made more dazzling discoveries in a very short time than in the whole past history of the human race has tempted him very strongly to turn his back on the Church he considers an impediment to progress, to live without God, to believe himself to be God.

Man has not yet realized how well Christianity, in spite of its limited horizons in the past, has prepared him for the amazing marvels of today and for the surprises that await us in the third millennium. For example, he has not, generally speaking, been struck by the circumstance that it is Western Christianity that is living through the technoscientific explosion of our time.

Men of today and tomorrow will see that the attitude of the Church is not a trick of artful insincerity, but only a deeper plunge into truths which were already present in the Gospel. Men of today and those of tomorrow will perceive that the Church does not fear the genuine advance of science but is willing, when necessary, to re-examine and sift to the bottom those affirmations made in the past which should be questioned now. It will not be long before man, who has already begun to live in the twenty-first century, will discover that science does not begin to exhaust the reality of human life. Let us suppose—and it does not seem absurd to me, for we have no reason to set limits to the generosity with which Our Father has made man a participant in His creative power—let us suppose that the co-creator, working in his laboratory, will succeed in creating life. It is not science or technology, but religion, which must ask what we are to do with this life.

To Pope John XXIII, man was still living on the first day of Creation. Before our astonished eyes he splits the atom, flings meteors into the sky, and makes ready for the first landings on the galloping stars in their courses.

Let us hope that humanity does not divide into armed camps and gamble with forces that tomorrow could lay waste the earth, just as these wonders are coming to pass. Let us hope that mankind can learn, in spite of its fear and trembling, that in the blackest darkness, in the gloomiest night, there is still a glimmer of light. May men, may all of us, brothers in greatness and misery, find hope again!

The Bible teaches us that when God created man in His image, He entrusted to him the mission of conquering nature and finishing the work of Creation.

There are those who are distressed at seeing men gain mastery over realms that once seemed the exclusive province of the Creator: splitting atoms, sowing stars, leaving earth behind and making ready to control the Universe, carrying out genetic mutations, performing marvelous feats with electronics, chemicals, and petroleum, and beginning to master automation.

Those who are frightened at seeing man grasp in a few years the knowledge he had not attained in previous millennia; those who ask in aggrieved wonder if man's hubris has no limits, are distressed because they think they are witnessing the defeat of God. So mean, so limited is human vision.

We have conceived the idea of a jealous, petty little God, afraid of His own shadow; one who insists on creating everything directly and personally, without dividing the gift of Creation with any of His creatures.

We falsify the idea of the true living God, and are then filled with fear when our half-truths and illusions crumble into dust. There are places where panic reigns even today at the mention of such facts as evolution and the true age of the Universe. . . .

There are apologists for the Church who, with the best intentions in the world, betray the essential meaning of religion: they must try to set up impassable barriers against the tide of change; they are motivated by prejudices which they believe to be dogmas; they set up for themselves, unwittingly and unwillingly, dreadful surprises and tests of their faith. If tomorrow man should travel freely through space and discover that the Creator is infinitely more powerful than we had imagined; if tomorrow man should make contact with other creatures— subhuman, human, or superhuman—then those who insist in the name of faith that life, or human life at least, exists only on earth, are in for a shock. If it should turn out to be part of the Divine Plan that one of God's creatures should resurrect the dead or shepherd the passing of matter from nonlife to life, whoever has set limits on the mighty plan of Creation will not know where to turn.

Fearless Christians can smile happily with John XXIII, and instead of thinking that the end of the world is near, be confident that they are witnesses to the first day of Creation.

While pessimists tremble with fear as the year 2000 approaches and in panic repeat hackneyed statistics about the demographic explosion, Vatican II Christians trust in God's power to work through man, His fellow creator.

It is true enough that those who like to moralize take delight in proving, and that quite easily, that man's spiritual progress has a long way to go before it catches up with the advance of technology and science, and that two-thirds of the human race is sinking ever more deeply into poverty and hunger while a tiny, privileged elite is daily attaining to a more luxurious affluence.

For the moment, let us be content with pointing out that the possibility of equable, harmonious development for the whole human race has ceased to be chimerical. By using only those forces available to us now, it is already within our power to conquer hunger, overcome misery, and achieve an even rate of development everywhere in the world.

It is curious, is it not, that not infrequently those who wish to make man the subject instead of the object of history are convinced that the only way to do so is to convert him to humanistic atheism. They are the ones Paul VI was thinking of when he said:

The religion of God become man has encountered the religion—for it is a religion—of man become God. And with what result? A collision? A struggle? Anathema? It might have been so, but it was not. The old story of the Good Samaritan fits the Council's spiritual cast of mind. It was penetrated through and through by a boundless sympathy. The discovery of human needs, which become greater as the sons of earth themselves become greater, absorbed the attention of our Synod. Concede us this merit at least, oh ye modern humanists who renounce all claim to the transcendence of Supreme Good; and recognize that our humanism is as modern as yours. We too, we more than anyone else, aspire to lift man above himself.

The Pope was applauding the New Humanism. Not new in the sense of its premises not being founded in Scripture; not new in the sense that only now is Biblical, Christian humanism being discovered. New only in the sense that man has now fallen heir both to powers never before attained or even imagined and to perils graver than any he has faced before; and since it is up to man to overcome those perils, the Holy Spirit is inspiring the Church to make its humanism explicit as never before and to embrace all the people of God in its plan of action.

It is worthwhile to attempt to trace some of the sweeping lines of the *new* Christian humanism.

Its first act is to welcome what is true in all other kinds of humanism, including atheistic humanism, no matter how one-sided and aggressive they may be. Just because there are those who virtually reduce man to a question of economic motivation, we should not ignore the place in human life that economics ought to fill. Just because there are those who see only the sexual nature of man, we should not forget the tremendous reality of sex. And the same is true of the thirst for knowledge, the desire for power, social trends, and many other partial truths which it is our duty to free from their relationship to ideologies often judged contrary to Christian thought.

The New Humanism recognizes man's right and duty to have dominion over the earth and to finish the task of Creation. It is aware that for the first time in history it is within man's power to sweep misery from the earth, that misery which is an outrage to humanity and an insult to the Creator. It sees that we are at a crossroads: either the victory will go to egoism, and a tiny parcel of mankind, a drop in the ocean, will grow richer and richer and sink deeper and deeper into hedonism while the rest of humanity is crushed; or we will realize we are brothers, not only in word but in deed, and then the human march through history will take an entirely new turn.

This is the challenge we face as Christians in the developing world. In order to meet this challenge there must be a meeting of minds between ourselves and the technologists, however removed they think they are from religious practices and even from the idea of God.

The subhuman masses are prone to attribute anything good that happens to them to Divine Mercy and interpret whatever ills befall them as divine punishment. Droughts, floods, plagues that decimate their cattle or lay waste their fields, the sicknesses man is heir to—all these are either a divine trial to test their fortitude, or a spell, the evil eye, the work of the Devil.

It is high time we purified the religion of the humble, reminding our brothers that of course God exists, that of course He has the power to intervene in the Universe and in human life at any time; but that it is also true, and crystal clear, that God has given man dominion over nature and the power to finish Creation by taming the natural forces of the world.

It is man's obligation to harness droughts and floods, to combat plagues and cure disease. This is in no way a diminution of God. Quite the contrary, it only enhances Him in our eyes. The more boldly man advances, the more his deeds will be a hymn to the glory of the Father-Creator.

The subhuman masses are also prone to lay at God's door evils that are really the fault of frailty, the spoiled fruits of our selfishness.

Severino of the Northeast, son of Severino, grandson of Severino, lives, like those other Severinos, a living death. He does not live; he vegetates. Not like a shady tree with its roots filled with the sap of life, but like his brother the cactus. So far he has not rebelled. From his illiterate parents and in the chapel belonging to his lord and master he learned to be patient, like the Son of God who was condemned unjustly and died on the Cross to save us. In his own way he concludes that things cannot be otherwise. A pupil in the school of Christianity and fatalism, he simply accepts the fact that some are born rich and others poor, and that such is the will of God.

Without stirring up hatred—which is never constructive, which cannot be Christian or even human—we have the duty to rectify and purify the religious views of the people.

It should be a source of shame to us that Brazil, a Christian country, was one of the last to free itself from slavery. It is time we fulfilled the emancipation proclamation we celebrate on every May 13. If the United States of America felt morally obligated to declare war on the poverty in which, as Lyndon Johnson courageously declared, thirty million North Americans are living, why should we be ashamed to confess that millions of Brazilians in our own Northeast, North, and Middle West live in subhuman conditions? How can we stand idly by while the masses seek false consolation for their own misery in a perverted view of Christian teaching which would justify those who think that religion is an opiate of the people? How can we consent to see the Church's teaching emptied of all social content and reduced to mere alms-giving, when this same teaching demands more and more imperiously that no human creature be left abandoned in a state of subhuman want?

I feel that there must be receptivity in the minds of everyone, especially technicians, to the new Christian humanism which leads us to the desire of proclaiming the true God by our every word and example. Not the ingenuous, spiteful, magic-working God of our superstitious poor, but the Creator and Father Who, far from mistrusting man, fearing His own shadow, and insisting on the prerogative of creating each separate being through His personal intervention—elephant and ant, star and worm—set creative evolution in motion and opened for the beings created in His image almost boundless opportunity to participate in His act of Creation.

Not the God of our fatalistic, subhuman masses, but the one true God Who, having created each and every man in His likeness, will not allow cactus-men, shadow-men, to exist side by side with men who are truly human.

But we must not forget that the technocrats at the apogee of technology also have need of religion.

Technology has need of faith if it is not to engender monsters. The only way we can avoid being devoured by the machines we create, or by the forces we unleash, or by the missiles and robots we bring into being, is through a high-minded, frank understanding between science and faith, which will then complement each other in a partnership of mutual respect.

All human beings, made in the image and likeness of God, have an innate longing for liberty. Liberty is not license. But since God Himself is the model, the first to respect the freedom He has given us, we cannot be contained within the bonds of suspicion, constraint, or surveillance.

Human thought longs to assert itself, and rebels when it is treated as if men were children, or at most adolescents.

Autonomy is vital to a university, for example. Universities and mistrust, universities and lack of freedom, excessive control, confinement, closed doors and windows, the absence of air and light, are mutually incompatible and can never coexist.

It so happens that the Church, in this new Vatican II phase, respects man, God's partner, as never before. In particular, it respects his thoughts. And now more than ever before, it has need of the university in the plenitude of its essential qualities, its power, and its mission.

Teilhard de Chardin is a faithful interpreter of the feelings of contemporary man:

When first we come face to face with the Universe, its dizzying dimensions fill us with terror and awe. As long as we believed that the earth was set in the center of a small number of spheres revolving around it in a fixed order, we could contemplate the heavenly infinitude of stars in serene admiration. But when our eyes behold this perfect order thrown askew, torn asunder, and flung explosively into space; when we begin to count in thousands of light-years and thousands of galaxies; and when, at the other extreme of astronomic vastness, the Immense reappears to our newly gained perception in the inconceivable anthill of the Infinitesimal; when the blindfold falls from our eyes, there arises in us a sense of awe and of nausea at our own insignificance. . . . To the two abysses of Pascal which we have now begun to sound—that within man and that without—two more have been added: the abyss of Numbers, the teeming flood of bodies and corpuscles which encompasses us, and the abyss of Time, the never-ending axis on which Space eternally turns and unfolds. What fixed ground then remains? Must we not feel annihilated, undone, in the heart of these vastnesses and these multitudes? The ever-lengthening shadow of cosmic Immensity darkens the soul of contemporary man.

Once recovered from that initial terror, a man regains his courage and pulls himself together for a new start. Nuclear energy? It is now only a question of economics. Man goes to work busily inventing ways to change the present scheme of life and labor and envisions, as a near reality, maximum production with minimum effort.

The building of servo-mechanisms creates a new enchanted world into which man dives headfirst. Missiles, robots, electronic brains do not frighten him because he believes they are under his complete control.

Once again, man does not stop to ask himself whether most of humanity may not become absolutely dependent on a little group of technocrats with power undreamed of by emperors in the age of absolute monarchy.

Man finds himself on the threshold of voyages into space, with all the dazzling surprises such flight may bring. He already perceives that in the third millennium psychoanalysis will quite probably be as exact a science as physics is now, and he foresees the possibility of controlling psychic energy.

Man already sees himself as an historical subject instead of an object. He went from ox to ox herd, and now the ox herd is a king!

It is easy to understand the temptation not only to do without God, but to usurp the very throne of the ancient of days, the Creator and Father.

God has taught the Church of Vatican II to trust man. Instead of judging him as conceited and rash, and losing patience with him when, with incredible daring, he rushes off in all directions, the Church exults and proclaims that by acting in this way man is only following the Divine command to rule nature and complete the work of Creation.

In other times the Church would have been alarmed to see the trend toward atheism that contemporary thought is taking—

an atheism which believes itself to be both constructive and organic, inevitable and natural. Today the Church perceives that behind the façade of contemporary atheism lies a wealth of humanistic yearning which it recognizes as a very positive force.

In other times the Church would have decreed that humanism without God is doubly atheistic. Today it perceives that all those who love their fellow creatures are obeying one of the two great commandments: that everyone who loves his neighbor and is concerned with his fulfillment and happiness, though he proclaim himself an atheist, is nevertheless doing the work of God.

The universities, especially the schools of philosophy and liberal arts, have an extremely important role to play at this time:

- To encourage man in his endeavors, trustingly, fearlessly, as one familiar with the Bible who has heard and heeded God's command to His fellow creator.
- To succor man when he is overcome by vertigo, in the hour when he learns the great De Lubac's profound lesson: "Man can, literally speaking, manage the earth without God, but humanism without God soon becomes inhuman, antihuman. . . ."
- To demonstrate to man that he need not banish God to be free. On the contrary, God wants him to be free and has given overwhelming proof that He respects man's freedom.
- To help man understand that his yearning to be God is a righteous yearning. Not in vain was he created in the Divine image. Not in vain has he been summoned to share our Father's creative powers.
- To bring Christ and contemporary man face to face.

It may be that never in the history of mankind have we been in a better position to understand Christ than today. Not a deformed, multilated, unrecognizable Christ, but Christ as the

Gospels show Him, Christ as He appears in the Epistles of St. Paul, so admirably echoed, in our time, in the voice of Teilhard de Chardin.

One of the chief concerns of Catholic universities today should be to establish a dialogue with atheists.

Atheism almost always arises from deficiencies in the lives and thoughts of believers.

I should like to mention here the names of three men who symbolize three different manifestations of contemporary atheism, or rather of atheistic humanism. All three represent what is most lofty and most worthy of respect and love in a world without faith: the evolutionist Julian Huxley, the psychoanalyst Erich Fromm, and the Marxist Roger Garaudy.

Let us try to make evolutionists see and feel that Christians have lost their fear of evolution and, at the same time, that evolutionism has much to gain by accepting the Creator and thus giving a new impulse to creative evolution. If it is true that man is self-conscious evolution, it is also true that man has the choice of either respecting or stifling his innate potentialities for freedom, creativity, and personal development. Forgive me if I insist once again: in twenty-first-century terms, show to men who thirst after Him that God Who became man because He so loved man.

Let us try to make psychoanalysts see and feel the need to re-examine the celebrated axiom: "Obsessive neurosis is a religious system, and religion a universal obsessive neurosis."

Let us make them see that Christianity is becoming less and less a religion of fear and more and more firmly one of trust and love. Let us show them how liturgical renewal shatters the parallel between ritual and neurotic patterning. Let us prove to them, above all, that we do not fear psychoanalysis as long as it rests on a solid foundation of truth; we have no difficulty in welcoming research into the existence of a specifically religious dynamic force inherent in the human psyche, or in facing the challenge of the theory of transference, with its reflections on morality and the whole interior life of man; or in discovering the compatibility between man's dynamic makeup and the concept of man as the image and likeness of God.

Let us make Marxists see and feel that Christianity has made a decision no longer to be or to appear to be "the opiate of the people." The Church has made up its mind no longer to be or appear to be alienated and alienating; it is the desire of the Church to become more and more incarnate in the world, like Christ Himself, whose work it does, and that this will in no way cause it to lose the transcendence that is its sign of divinity.

Let us remind them that only a short time ago Pope Paul VI urged the bishops of Latin America to make a sincere effort to see that the Church takes an active part in the development and integration of this continent.

As for me, if I were asked to name the task, the mission most appropriate to us, I would not hesitate to say: let us try to be witnesses to Vatican II—living examples of open, constructive, confident, courageous Christianity; Christians in name and deed; Christian adults.

3

The Church in the World

It is a serious responsibility to live in the time of the Ecumenical Council, Vatican II.

Pope John XXIII hoped that this Council would be different from its predecessors. He stated openly that it would not be a condemning Council—and added with a smile that the errors it might have condemned were sufficiently damned already.

No, the task of this Council was to reform a Church divine in origin but entrusted to frail and sinful men. As Pope John saw it, the Church through its own self-renewal and reform will unite Christian families and draw to it all men of good will.

To priests, religious, and laymen in this Archdiocese I propose that we be guided by the Council's example. Instead of being so eager to reform others, let us first make a serious effort to bring about our own revival.

The difference between the saint and the Pharisee is essentially this: the Pharisee is indulgent toward himself and rigid toward others; he would like to drive everyone to heaven by force. The saint demands much of himself, but toward sinners he is as generous as Divine goodness itself, as boundless in his mercy as our Father in heaven.

To those who dwell in what is conventionally called the world, I wish to repeat here Pope Paul's truly inspired words in the opening speech of the Second Session of Vatican II:

Let the world know that the Church looks upon it with profound understanding, with sincere admiration, with the honest intention not to overcome it but to serve it; not to scorn it but to realize its worth; not to condemn it but to comfort and save it.

Before passing from theory to practice, before facing reality in the Northeast within the broader reality that conditions it, prudence requires that we lay to rest certain suspicions which border on calumny: has the Church indeed abandoned heavenly truth for earthly reality? Has it embraced the ephemeral, thus abandoning the eternal or relegating it to a place in the background? Has it forgotten original sin and come to believe in the natural goodness of man?

Not at all. The essential question for us was, is, and always will be the story of salvation: God created man in His own image; man used his divine gifts of intelligence and freedom against his Creator and Father; instead of abandoning man, the Heavenly Father sent His Son, God made man, Jesus Christ, to save all men.

Two loves—love of God and love of mankind—are one and the same. We are deceiving ourselves if we think we can love God, Whom we cannot see, without loving man, whom we do see. And man is not only a soul, he is also a body, spirit inseparably embodied in matter. By living in time, we pass through the door to eternity.

The struggle for economic development is Christian, profoundly Christian, as long as it is a synonym for brotherly love, for helping to rescue from misery millions of fellow creatures now existing in a subhuman state.

Of course we do not and shall not forget the necessity of imposing an ethic and a mystique on this struggle for development to save it from becoming merely a passage from the degrading misery that disfigures the divine image in ourselves to a slough of ephemeral, dehumanizing, pagan life.

Human alienation can take place through neglect of the eternal in pursuit of the temporal as well as through neglect of the temporal in pursuit of the eternal.

These are the two faces of alienation.

If Marx had seen around him a Church incarnate, sprung from Christ's incarnation; if he had lived among Christians who expressed, by their deeds and the truths they lived by, a love of mankind as the highest expression of their love of God; if he had lived in the days of Vatican II, which has embraced the best sayings and teachings of Marx's theology of earthly reality, he would not have condemned religion as the opiate of the people and the Church as an alienated and alienating force.

Economics is not the only reality. Man's transcendental thirst is another, and just as real; so are his thirst for unity, for the true, the beautiful, and the good; his thirst for the eternal and infinite; his thirst for the absolute. Nor is that all: there is occurring today an historical process of singular relevance. At this moment when man, having lived twenty millennia in the space of twenty years, believes himself to be only a step away from becoming a *god,* it is a good time to remind him that God became man in order to make the divinity of man a reality.

The Church must concern itself with the new man who is about to be born and with the meaning of social evolution. It is just here that the Christian idea of man may help us to find a solution. The new man cannot be merely a glorified producer-consumer, a cog in a mechanistic society, though he gain dominion over all of nature external to himself. The goal to strive for is a *free* and *conscious* being, progressively freed from a thousand kinds of servitude so that his inalienable freedom can flourish and he will be truly free, free even from himself, free to give himself to others. Thus a society of free men with respect for one another will be perfected through the selfless giving of ourselves to our neighbors.

The role of the Church in Latin-American development can be effective only if it is part of an effort that involves the whole world. The social revolution the world is crying out for demands the unceasing conversion of individuals and whole peoples. Who among us does not need to be converted, and converted again and again? Which of us stands in no need of constant rebirth? The question holds not only for individuals but for nations: all of us, without exception, are in need of constant conversion. The world is not divided into innocent and sinful nations. Our sins take different forms, but all of them—those of nations as well as those of individuals—are rooted in selfishness.

The social revolution of which the world stands in need will not come about through an armed coup, or guerrilla skirmishes, or war. It must be a profound and radical change requiring Divine Grace and a world movement to change public opinion, a movement which can and should be helped and encouraged by the Church, in Latin America and everywhere else. Nothing can be built on hate. And a whole new world is waiting to be built.

Such action is all the more urgent since some of the best, the most idealistic and purest of men, especially among the young, are losing patience and letting themselves be carried away by movements of radical violence.

Since the day of the Discovery, Latin-American society has grown and developed under the influence of the Church. Its social, economic, political, and cultural structure was forged in the molds of Iberian Christianity; and our wars of independence made no material change in our societies. Only now, for the first time, are we witnessing the prelude of substantial change. The Church is indissolubly linked to this historical past, with its true values, its authentic achievements, and its crowning moments of glory—and its failures, its false values, its aberrations.

This fact burdens the Church with an indisputable responsibility to confront these new challenges, and makes demands upon it which can no longer be denied. The Church must not allow the authentic values of our civilization, which she helped to create, to be swept away by the avalanche of imminent structural change. But the Church is also called upon to condemn our collective sins and unjust and unresponsive social structures, not as an outside judge, but as one who acknowledges her share of responsibility and guilt. The Church must find the courage to acknowledge that she is a part of that past in order to recognize more deeply her responsibility for the present and the future.

Whatever may have been the course of history in the past, today the Church is an effective presence in the development of Latin America. This human situation, this society in crisis, demands that she search her conscience and make a determined effort to help the continent free itself from the shackles of underdevelopment.

In order to carry out this mission, a radical effort of purification and conversion is demanded of the Church. Her relationships with the underdeveloped masses, with the most diverse social groups, with organizations of all kinds, should be more and more often relationships in which she is a servant. Her strength must derive less and less from prestige and power and more and more from the strength of the Gospel at the service of mankind. By taking this road she will reveal to the men of this continent in torment the true countenance of Christ.

This demand implies a thorough renovation of parochial and diocesan structure and of all Catholic institutions; of the relationships among bishops, religious, and laymen, and of the religious orders, congregations, and colleges. Proclaiming the message of the Gospel, bringing new Christians into the fold, celebrating the liturgy and carrying on ecumenical dialogue, all must take on new dimensions. Most significantly, all must be steeped in the human reality of a continent struggling to develop its resources. We must not think of the Church as standing above the fray and merely extending its good offices to the cause of development. To do so would be to stop at half-measures, without ever reaching the crux of the problem. It is the Church herself, her most intimate mystery, which is called to self-renewal.

In the process she will find her own proper forms of expression, her own originality, the Divine Grace at the heart of the Universal Church. Only through such an all-inclusive, integrated renovation of every aspect of her life, through placing herself at the service of mankind, can the Church meet today's historical challenge.

Have you thought what it will mean to those skilled in the techniques of development to find the Church in underdeveloped areas helping the masses to become men, leading them to overcome their fatalism, reminding them that while God does exist and obviously has the right to intervene in His Creation, it was God Himself who gave man the right and duty to have dominion over nature and complete the work of Creation?

Have you thought what it will mean to development technicians to feel the effects of a theology of development which teaches that we have no right to take the easy way out and saddle God with responsibility for *everything*, which inculcates the courage to defy the inclemency of nature and above all to shoulder full responsibility for social problems?

Instead of contenting ourselves with watching people hold processions to beg for rain when there is a drought, and other processions to beg for the rain to stop when there is a flood, we will teach from one end of this continent to the other that droughts and floods are problems we must solve ourselves by technical means, by the use of intelligence, courage, discipline, and honesty.

Instead of letting people repeat in their terrible resignation that "some are born rich and others poor: it's God's will" (and we know what grievous exploitation such phrases can cover), let us openly declare that the social and economic structures of Latin America are unjust and must be replaced by others which are more just, *more humane*. Only then will we have the right to affirm that there are no slaves in this country or on this continent.

What a relief it must have been to those who were dubbed subversive and Communist simply because they expressed a hunger and thirst for justice, to hear the Pope make such a statement as this:

No one has an unconditional, absolute right to own private property. The earth belongs to all, not only to the rich.

No one has the right to reserve for his exclusive use more than he needs, while others lack the necessities of life.

The development experts know very well why Pope Paul VI spoke in this way, the deep reasons he had for doing so, and the fearless resolution he revealed.

Did the Pope speak too hastily? Did he launch an irresponsible, one-sided encyclical? This unjust, unfounded accusation has arisen in areas which do not even perceive how one-sided their own lives are. The dread of Communism, when it becomes an obsession, blinds people to the horrors of a social system which enshrines profit as the all-powerful engine of economic progress; competition as the supreme law of economics; and private ownership of the means of production as an absolute right, without limits or corresponding social obligations.

Many people, for obvious reasons, cannot understand why the Pope should have accused liberal capitalism of being the motivating force of international financial imperialism; but it is hardly necessary to point out the significance of the international trusts in the world today.

At first glance the number of business firms in any developed country seems to be great, but to all eyes except those of the gullible, their number is actually shrinking to a mere handful of corporations, an all-powerful economic nucleus linked, of course, to small economic nuclei in the other industrialized countries, a gigantic web enmeshing the underdeveloped world in its toils.

These are the real masters of the world, the cold and calculating manipulators of war and peace (more frequently war), the implacable wheelers and dealers of international finance. It is not easy for the disseminators of the news to escape their power. From them emanate imponderable influences which exert dangerous control over the written and spoken press, over governments, universities, and even—why try to deny it?—

over religious institutions, which are always in need of aid for their apostolic and social undertakings. Woe to him who dares stand up and point an accusing finger at these forces: he runs the risk of disappearing from the scene without even the consolation of knowing that the murderous plot will be exposed, for by strange coincidence all the witnesses will have died one by one.

The author of *Populorum Progressio* well knows where the excesses of economic dictatorship lead.

Rerum Novarum, which examined labor contracts and considered the fact that between all-powerful corporation heads and defenseless workers any possibility for real dialogue was minimal and the workers' freedom of action was practically nil, served to remind us that the workers' consent is not sufficient to ensure a just contract. It is necessary to substitute the claims of natural law for the rule of freedom of consent, which on the part of the workers was often more apparent than real.

The new encyclical recognizes that individual or collective injustices of the past have now assumed global dimensions. Proletariat nations are at the mercy of affluent nations; or rather, to be more just and more exact, at the mercy of groups which, in rich nation and proletariat nation alike, are more powerful, not only than feeble states, but than even the very strongest.

An encyclical like *Populorum Progressio* was not intended to be praised, applauded, and then forgotten; it was meant to produce results, to have repercussions in the realm of practical affairs. One of the recurring themes in Pope Paul's letter to his flock is the idea that time is running against us.

What is to be done, then? Shall we wait until reforms have been carried out, and then and only then bring social awareness to the masses? The idea of waiting is absurd, impossible, particularly for the Church, which must assume much of the responsibility for the present crisis. We are in no danger of acting too hastily: we are already several centuries late.

Should we, then, first try to bring social awareness to the

elite, the managerial, governing, entrepreneurial classes, and then and only then speak to the people? There is no time to waste: the two acts of social consciousness, of *conscientização*, must be simultaneous.

Already there are those who have abandoned hope in democratic solutions because laws are passed and never implemented; bureaus are set up to carry out the laws, but there are imponderable forces which virtually cancel out the effectiveness of even those institutions which are run by trained professionals eager to get on with the job.

I do not believe in violence, I do not believe in hatred, I do not believe in armed insurrections. They take place too quickly: they change the circumstances of men's lives without giving them time to adapt to the changes. It is useless to dream of reforming the socioeconomic structure, the outer structure, of our lives as long as there is not a correspondingly deep change in our inner selves. And this is the conversion to which Pope Paul alluded in the United Nations.

But while I do not believe in armed violence, I am scarcely so naïve as to think that brotherly counsel and pathetic appeals are enough to make socioeconomic structures tumble like the walls of Jericho.

In the hope of avoiding otherwise inevitable explosions tomorrow, we plan specifically to organize democratic pressure groups to operate within the law but, within the limits of the law, to risk everything. These groups will be organized in accordance with technical criteria and efficiency, but will leave no room for infiltrators to use them for their advantage.

Such work would be unspeakably rash if we did not at the same time consult technical experts who can not only provide us with ammunition in the form of data which will make our arguments unanswerable, but, most importantly, can point out technical solutions to problems outside our field of competence.

Allow me to remind those who are scandalized to see a bishop meddling in matters which may seem to be none of his business that the Church, in its most solemn documents, feels called upon to examine economic matters of grave importance to human kind.

In *Mater et Magistra* Pope John XXIII gave precious admonitions concerning the relations between the developed and the underdeveloped worlds. This is the text:

Those economically developed states giving aid to developing countries should be very careful to resist the temptation to take advantage of this form of technical and financial cooperation to obtain political advantages. If aid is given with a view to domination, it should be publicly denounced, for it means the establishment of a new type of colonialism—veiled, no doubt, but no less powerful than that from which numerous political communities have only recently freed themselves. This would result in unsettled international relations and constitute a menace and a peril to world peace.

In spite of the transcendence of the great *Mater et Magistra* encyclical, it stops short—at the time when it was written it could not do otherwise—with the hope that countries abundantly provided for would increase their aid to countries that were economically weak.

Now the Ecumenical Council, Vatican II, in its Pastoral Constitution on the role of the Church in the world, states unhesitatingly that in the relations between the two worlds, the developed and the underdeveloped, aid is not enough: what is needed is a thorough revision of international trade policies.

The following data justify Pope John's concern and fully confirm the validity of the position adopted by the Council.

We have at hand the new Prebisch Report, prepared for the Second United Nations Conference on Trade and Development. It reflects the melancholy end of the First Decade of Development proclaimed by the United Nations for 1960–1970. Raúl Prebisch has some dismal statistics to report. We should use them as our starting point, and from there go on to find new bases of courage, hope, and optimism.

From 1960 to 1965, average per capita income in the developed countries rose from $1,400 to $1,700; in the underdeveloped countries, the figures were $132 and $142.

Agricultural progress in the developing countries was disappointing: efforts to increase production were hampered not only by an explosive population increase but by institutionalized obstacles such as archaic agrarian structures, ill-conceived credit schemes, and inadequate marketing systems.

In the mid-1930's, eleven million tons of grain were exported by the underdeveloped countries; now those same countries are importing thirty million tons a year.

The developed countries tend to make less and less use of the raw materials exported by the underdeveloped countries. As one example among many, let us take cotton. From 1957 to 1961, the developed nations were still importing 27 percent of the cotton they needed. In 1965 the figure was down to 17 percent. It now takes only 40 hours for machines to do the work which took 130 hours in 1960. The two and a half acres which produced 268 pounds of cotton then now produce 500. But between 1955 and 1964 the percentage of artificial fibers used by the garment industry grew from 26 percent to 38 percent.

A recent study of import tariffs shows that the average nominal *ad valorem* tariffs charged by developed countries on manufactured products actually vary according to the origin of those products: the average is 11 percent when they come from other developed countries, but 17 percent when they come from the underdeveloped world.

The external financial vulnerability of the developing countries became more dangerously acute precisely during the decade of development. In 1948 the correlation between those countries' reserves and the value of their imports was approximately 70 percent. By 1965 it had fallen to 30 percent. And day by day it becomes increasingly apparent that changes in world monetary systems will be made without the least participation by the developing world.

It was resolved in the United Nations that the developed

countries should guarantee the underdeveloped countries financial resources to the amount of one percent of their respective gross national product, but the developed world has never reached this minimum—this bare, pitiful minimum—of one percent. In 1961 the percentage was 0.87 percent. In 1964, instead of going up it went down, to 0.66 percent, and nevertheless by that year the total indebtedness of the underdeveloped countries had reached the figure of $38 billion, plus $4 billion interest.

We must not allow the developed world to delude itself or try to delude us by endeavoring, for example, to raise the level of its aid to developing countries from 0.66 percent to one, or even two or three, percent. We cannot allow our grave concern at the course humanity is taking to be diverted in this simplistic and self-indulgent manner, as if it were a question of ideological prejudice against any one people or country. The systematic bleeding of the underdeveloped world is readily apparent when one compares what the underdeveloped countries receive in investment from the wealthy countries with the return to those countries on such investments.

According to official U.S. statistics, between 1950 and 1961 the total amount of liquid American capital exported was $13.7 billion. During the same period of time, the total liquid capital imported was $23.2 billion. But American assets in the underdeveloped world between 1950 and 1961 increased by $22.9 billion, climbing dizzily from $11.8 billion to $34.7 billion. The injustice becomes starkly apparent when one compares the aid sent to underdeveloped countries with the amount they lose as a result of the wretched prices imposed on raw materials imported from the Third World. In the case of Latin America, that loss has been calculated to amount to $10.1 billion in the decade between 1950 and 1961.

4

Christianity, Communism, and Democracy

Universal solidarity is one of the main recurring themes in *Populorum Progressio*. In the opening words of the encyclical (No. 1) Pope Paul VI proclaims the decision of the Church, consciously arrived at after the examination of conscience that was Vatican II, to serve mankind by taking upon herself the duty of helping men to realize the urgent need for joint action, for unity at this decisive crossroads in human history.

A little farther on he confesses:

As the heirs of past generations and the beneficiaries of the work of our contemporaries, we have obligations toward all, and we must take an interest in those who will come after us to widen the circle of the human family. Universal solidarity is not only a benefit to us when realized; it is our duty to bring it about.

As we know, the whole second part of *Populorum Progressio* expresses the Pope's longing for united human efforts toward development.

Remarking on the duty of the more favored peoples (No. 44), the encyclical says that their obligations are rooted in human spiritual brotherhood and are presented in the triple aspect of a duty of human solidarity, a duty of social justice, and a duty of universal charity, all helping to form a more human world for us all, a world in which all will give and all will receive, and the progress of some will be no obstacle to the development of others. The passage concludes by stating: "The question is a grave one, for the future of world civilization is at stake."

Without fear of repeating himself, the Pope again speaks of the duty of peoples (No. 48) and calls it "very solemn," affirming that "no nation has the right to keep its wealth for its own exclusive use: . . . each country must produce more and better goods in order to give its own people a truly human standard of living and, at the same time, contribute to the concerted development of human society."

Populorum Progressio faces squarely the obstacles to world unity: exaggerated nationalism (No. 62) and racism (No. 63); it expresses hopefulness (No. 64) that the less developed countries will achieve working common markets that will enable them to participate effectively in the universal dialogue.

To quote Pope Paul:

World solidarity, ever more effective, should enable all peoples to feel that they themselves are the authors of their destiny. The past was often marked by relations of brute force among nations; the day is dawning when international relations will rest on mutual respect and friendship, cooperative interdependence, and a common advancement for which each bears responsibility.

In this century of dialogue, the Pope makes a point of reminding us (No. 37) that: "Among civilizations as among persons, sincere dialogue fosters brotherhood."

According to *Populorum Progressio*, now is the time to act (No. 80):

The survival of countless innocent children, access to a more human way of life for countless unfortunate families, world peace and the future of civilization are imperiled.

Faced with this central idea of the encyclical, this tormenting preoccupation of Paul VI, let us try to work out three lines of agreement, each of which may contribute from a different angle to the cause of the universal unity which would almost seem to be the true purpose of *Populorum Progressio*. Humanity cannot help benefiting from the triple rapprochement which we will examine here:

- Between the so-called Christian world and the Socialist world.
- Between the developed and the underdeveloped worlds.
- Among all the religions of the world, in a definitive broadening of ecumenism.

When most of the Greco-Latin world became Christian after three centuries of persecution; when the Christians left their catacombs for the dangerous splendor of the basilicas and the imperial court, the uproar of the approaching barbarians was already growing louder. An odd word: barbarians! It expressed all the complacent self-satisfaction of the Greeks and Romans, and at the same time their fear of losing a civilization which had once seemed invincible.

Nothing better epitomizes the feeling of that time than the anguish and panic of the great St. Augustine, whose vision, though that of a genius, could not perceive the ultimate meaning of what seemed to him a catastrophe, but in reality was the beginning of a new world. We are inevitably reminded of this historical episode by the attitude which the Western world has assumed toward the Socialist world. And "Western world," in the case of the liberal-capitalist or neo-capitalist nations, really means one which makes a show of being Christian when that suits its purposes.

The Socialist world has left itself open to attacks by the West. The Marxism which is its philosophy is, or seems to be, a synonym for materialism, hostile to religion as the supreme "alienated and alienating force." Atheism in the U.S.S.R. was militant, aggressive, and official. With the lowering of the Iron Curtain, it was very easy to watch the crushing of human rights, to feel the climate of denunciation and terror. There were uprisings, bloodily suppressed, and the Wall of Shame is still standing.

But then when Red China appeared on the scene, the Soviet Union was made to look almost moderate and rational.

The West has created, and tried to disseminate as widely as possible, several myths about Communism which are by no means easy to uproot:

- Anti-Communism is preached as the crusade of our time.

- The Soviet Union is held up as public enemy number one of freedom, democracy, and Christian civilization; the enemy of God, family, and native land. In many imaginations the Russians have come to occupy the place of horror and scorn which was once the lot of the Jews as a people guilty of deicide. . . . To some the U.S.S.R. has lately become public enemy number two, since Communist China goes far beyond it in the urge to dominate and destroy.

- And to balance the U.S.S.R. and China, the United States appears on the scene as the paladin of Christian civilization, democracy, and freedom. There are many who consider the Americans the new Chosen People, since they twice saved the world. Many see them as having restored the European economy after World War II and propelled the Third World onto the path of development. Many are only too grateful to recognize the right and duty of the United States to intervene in any country which finds itself in danger of going Communist, and consider just and righteous any and all economic and even military measures when it comes to barring Communist expansion. Many can accept any kind of war waged by North Americans and, with the best will in the world, manage to understand and accept escalating warfare and even, if that is inevitable, some new Hiroshima or Nagasaki.

This sort of mentality only serves to dig a more and more impassable moat between the Socialist world and the West, which is called Christian. By clinging to such myths we are making inevitable a third world war, with all its unforeseeable consequences for humanity. If we continue to look at the world through this sort of spectacles, it will be practically impossible for us to believe in the necessity, the urgent necessity, for world unity.

Let us have the courage and objectivity to recognize that error exists on both sides:

• As *Populorum Progressio* points out, even liberal capitalism has materialistic roots and is directly responsible for the rise of an international dictatorship of economic power.

• Why should we not encourage the efforts of Communist thinkers who, since they no longer consider Marxism a philosophy, a closed system, are rebelling against doctrines like those of Stalin, are rebelling against dogmatic, monolithic Marxism and condemning all the atrocities committed against peoples who only aspired to retain their own character and wanted their right of self-determination to be respected?

• Why not recognize that there is no longer just one type of Socialism and put in a plea for Christians to break free from adverse connotations of the term? It is not necessarily linked to materialism and by no means necessarily implies a regime which crushes human beings or the community; it can also mean a regime which serves the community and mankind.

Let us not allow ourselves to be blinded by political passion. Let us not confuse the clash of economic interests with holy wars or ideological battles.

The plain truth is that there has been selfishness on both sides as regards the deepest interests of the Third World. As an example, take the insensitivity of the Soviet Union, matched only by that of the United States, as demonstrated in the United Nations Conference on Trade and Development. The truth is that both sides are lacking in proper respect for the self-determination of peoples: there have been military occupations; there have been atrocities.

How long will Latin America meekly accept the imposed excommunication of her sister Cuba? Those who arose in Cuba only wanted to see her break free of her misery and underdevelopment. They first appealed for help to Canada and the United States. Those who leave a people cornered and at bay are responsible for whatever follies they may commit.

Some will answer that a dialogue with Cuba will expose Latin America to the terrible danger of Cubanization. But how long must democracy fear to take part in such dialogues? How long will it be before we open our eyes, shake off our naïveté, and realize that by isolating Cuba, by punishing her for the crime of wanting to exercise that self-determination which in theory we boast of respecting, we are only abandoning her to fall into the orbit of Soviet imperialism and thus creating, especially among our youth, the myth of Cuba as a model of revolution and a breaker of the bonds of underdevelopment?

An effective rapprochement between East and West would be of enormous help in effecting a rapprochement between North and South, that is, between the developed and the underdeveloped worlds. And what once seemed a utopian hope of unity may soon become reality as a result of the impasse the world has reached with regard to war:

• No one is quite mad enough to set off a thermonuclear war, now that nuclear bombs are no longer a monopoly and all the consequences of radioactivity are known.

• Local wars are becoming more costly in money and in human lives than world wars.

The peoples of the world are having to rethink their old assumptions. There will be a growing dissatisfaction at seeing economic interests masked by ideological pretexts. There will inevitably be attacks against the international trusts; for humanity cannot be expected to court destruction by letting itself be maneuvered by the cold masters of the world, the manipulators of peace and, above all, of war. It will become shameful to commit inhuman atrocities in the name of defending the free world. Men will understand that no less important than the wars that have already broken out is the greater war now in the process of gestation: if development is the new name for peace, then keeping 80 percent of the world in a state of underdevelopment and starvation is to hatch the most terrible of wars.

When the myths concocted against the Socialist world are seen for what they are—and when simultaneously the myths concocted in the Socialist world against the West are destroyed —this disarmament of minds will truly lead to the end of the suicidal arms race, to the general proscription on the use of atoms to wage war, and to a genuine respect for the right of all peoples to self-determination.

The development of the Third World is in the best interests of the developed world. It is not only a question of preventing an explosion of misery and the exploitation of underdevelopment.

In the short run, and for shortsighted politicians, it may be in the U.S. interest to prevent deep and rapid change in Latin America; it may be to their advantage to keep the human masses in a subhuman state, so long as a social pseudo-order is preserved and the internal security of the United States is not disturbed. In the long run, for farsighted and intelligent statesmen, it is in the interests of the United States that Latin America have the power to buy and trade. The same is true of Europe vis-à-vis Africa, or of the Soviet Union, Japan, and Continental China vis-à-vis Asia.

When warfare has ceased—and I insist on reminding you that political realism may lead men to embrace the ideal of peace much sooner than we think—and when, as a result, the arms race has ceased, the technology of the North, impelled by the necessity for full employment and as a servant of interests that go far beyond petty immediacy, will bring about the birth, expansion, and perfection of technology in the South.

Am I mad, or dreaming? Unless I am sadly mistaken, what appears fantastic is nourished by very concrete, very real facts. And so when we go back to *Populorum Progressio,* we are overjoyed to find it much more realistic than it once seemed. We are closer than we may imagine to a civilization of harmony and unity.

Of what will humanity not be capable when the development race takes the place of the arms race; when instead of decreasing in unnatural ways the number of human guests at the table of life, the head of each family is able to guarantee a human standard of living to children born in responsible marriage; when we can really speak of the infinitude of atoms as the servants of peace; when we no longer reason in terms of false surplus production but produce in order to do away, once and for all, with underconsumption?

Am I forgetting that selfishness will be a part of man to the end of time? Am I forgetting that sin entered the world and still casts its sinister shadow?

Well, I do hope, at least, for a respite. My generation has already witnessed two world wars and come within a hairsbreadth of a third. War has become a greater absurdity and folly than ever, now that whole cities are laid waste and whole civil populations exterminated, now that it is quite possible that humanity itself may be destroyed. And this power of destruction coexists with a capacity to build, to guarantee every human being a human standard of living.

What use are we making of the tremendous power of the press, radio, television, movies, theater? What use are we making of our teaching establishments, our universities especially? Why not try to join these tremendous forces and place them at the service of peace and justice and world unity?

It would be of far-reaching importance, not only to the rapprochement between East and West but to the ideal of universal solidarity, if among all religions there were mutual respect, and much more than that, an inner laying down of arms, a genuine good will. Ideally, all religions should join forces and agree on a joint program of action in the cause of justice and peace, of development and universal harmony.

The Catholic Church and the World Council of Churches are ripe for such unified effort. But a union of brothers in Christ is not enough. We should aim for a similar alliance with all the non-Christian religions, beginning with those that are fundamental not only to the cessation of present wars or those about to break out, but also to the conquest of underdevelopment in Asia and Africa: Judaism, Islam, and Buddhism.

Religion is held by Marxists to be the great alienated and alienating force. Let us be honest enough to admit that when our thoughts are on eternal life it is easy to forget the importance of life on earth; with our thoughts on social order, we do not always perceive that order in the underdeveloped world is often enough a synonym for injustice and stratified lack of order; with our thoughts on the undesirability of deep, rapid, jarring change, we use and abuse prudence to excess, and have more often been a brake than an accelerator. To carry honesty to its logical conclusion, let us admit that there is a subconscious factor that clouds our judgment and has been and still is a temptation to us: the circumstance that from wealthy men and governments we receive valuable aid for our social work, and often for our worship, too.

May God grant that all religions pass through the renewal now being effected in the Catholicism of Vatican II. One immediate result has been at least a desire to imitate Christ more closely and to try to serve instead of being served. The Catholic Church intends to be a servant and to become poor.

Of equal importance is the decision to enter the world. Instead of sinning by omission, instead of judging and condemning from afar, instead of remaining a spectator, the Church desires to take on flesh as Christ did, assuming all the joys and hopes, all the problems and yearnings, of men.

The bishops of this continent decided in Mar del Plata to see that the Church played an active role in the development and economic integration of Latin America. If it is true that in the past our preaching, catechism, and liturgy led consciously or unconsciously to conformity and kept the masses in a subhuman condition, the Catholic Church is now willing to adopt a new attitude from one end of the continent to the other, one in consonance with a developmental theology capable of becoming an extraordinary force for development.

Christian anthropology teaches us to encourage man to think

of himself as a partner in Creation, to behave not as an object
but as a subject of history; to break out of his discouragement,
apathy, and fear and take action as a Steward of God with the
mission to conquer nature and complete the work of Creation.
The vision of Christ's Incarnation is for Christians a living lesson in Christian commitment.

We will not remain satisfied with the sort of rebirth which
leads only to a more active and agreeable sort of catechism: we
want that catechism to discover in the Christian Message truths
that will help the masses become men and truths that will convert the rich made insensitive by their wealth.

We will not remain satisfied with the sort of liturgical renovation that makes a few changes in the altar and allows the
faithful to join in the singing and the prayers: we want the
liturgy to support the doctrine and give it deeper meaning,
elevating the humble and humbling the self-love of the powerful. But our allusions to the wind of renewal blowing through
the Catholic world do not mean that the contributions which
could and should be made by other religious groups are to be
forgotten.

If religion is to work on a global scale toward the ideal of
human solidarity, then those of us who bear the responsibility
of our belief in God are under obligation to set an example of
unity and the fair exchange of ideas.

I dream of an invitation from the Pontifical Commission for
Justice and Peace to those departments in any and all religions
which correspond to the World Council of Churches in the
evangelical sects. I dream of a congress in which each religion
will describe, in a clear and objective way, what truths it has
discovered in its own message which might advance the humani-
zation of the world: the defeat of egoism, the attainment of
peace and justice and world unity.

In this meeting of ecumenism without bounds there would
be room for agnostics and atheists who act in truth, who hunger
and thirst for a peace based on justice, for a world marked by

love—agnostics and atheists who are Christian in their deeds.

Are there premature and dangerous premises in this fraternal message?

It is fairly easy to agree on suggestions for a meeting of minds
between the developed and the underdeveloped worlds and
among the world's religions. More vulnerable to misunderstanding and attack is our longing for a rapprochement between East
and West, and above all our allusion to Cuba.

I know there will be no lack of critics—especially among
those who are more Christian than the Pope and who make of
anti-Communism a political resource and way of life—who will
find in these words a profession of devotion to Communism
and an aid to the Cubanization of this country, unconsciously
given, perhaps, and doubtless the result of some subtle maneuver
on the part of Fidel Castro's agents.

But enough of treating Brazil as if its underdevelopment were
intellectual as well as economic. There is no longer any rational
reason, only fuzzy-mindedness, in branding as subversive and
Communist anyone who hungers for justice and peace; anyone
who refuses to limit the world to the two options of capitalism
or Communism, as if a reluctance to embrace capitalism, or
any disagreement with the United States, were synonymous with
embracing Communism and becoming a satellite of the Soviet
Union or China.

In case of possible emergencies, allow me to identify myself.
I am a human being who considers himself a brother to all men,
without exception; a Christian who knows that Jesus Christ
did not die for Christians only, but for all men of every race,
creed, and ideology; a bishop who thanks God for the most
human figures of Pope John XXIII and Pope Paul VI; a bishop
who exults with *Populorum Progressio* and will be glad to make
sacrifices for world unity, desiring it not alone in words and
vague sentiments, but as a concrete and real unity, attained by
rapprochement among all religions, a drawing together of North
and South, of East and West.

The bugaboo of Communism is always useful to fall back on. It's an easy scarecrow to maneuver. After all, Popes have condemned atheistic Communism. After all, it is a fact that Communism is expanding throughout the world.

Nothing is easier than to wave the banner of anti-Communism against those who, even if they are not linked to the Party or to Communist ideology, have the audacity to discover materialistic roots in capitalism also; to observe that in reality neither "Socialism" nor "capitalism" can be used in the singular any longer; to point out that it is not Communism which is the gravest social problem in today's world, but another which is far graver and more explosive—the widening gap between the developed and the underdeveloped worlds; to go beyond the concept of social-welfare work and fight for the advancement to humanity of the billions of human beings who live in a sub-human state; and to dare to affirm that the relations between rich countries and starving countries are out of kilter, that it is not a question of aid to be increased, but of justice to be done, and that on a world-wide scale.

Anti-Communism is no less intolerant than Communism itself. It will admit no options but its own. And on the pretext of defending human beings, it is not above making contradictory use of processes that outrage human dignity, such as incitements to denounce others, arrests on mere suspicion, and physical and moral torture. What it does not see is that in so doing it is furnishing the Communists with propaganda by identifying as "Communist" any attitude of courage, intelligence, or daring in defense of truth and justice.

Let us discredit any and all attempts to distort our intentions, our thoughts, or our words, We are democrats, and we are using democratic processes, pure and simple. We believe in the power of ideas. We want to persuade, not only to prevail. Far from inciting hatred among workers for their employers, we want to awaken the consciences of both employers and workers at the same time, in order to obtain from both parties the prodigy of recognizing each his own obligations, a good starting point for the recognition of the rights of others.

It is important to recognize both our rights and duties if we are fully to respect the order instilled by the Creator, that indispensable condition for the establishment and consolidation of the peace on earth for which men of all times and places have profoundly longed. What are our duties with regard to justice? How far, for example, should men in general, and those in authority in particular, carry their defense of the fundamental rights of man?

It is not out of place to remind ourselves what those universal, inviolable, inalienable rights are. If we see them ignored, denied, trampled before our eyes, are we to fold our arms? If there is an obligation to act, is it up to us to defend right by force, or is there some valid, peaceful process by which right may be affirmed and so prevail?

Let no one be alarmed: it is not hate but love I preach. I am stubborn enough to prefer democratic methods to cabals and guerrillas. In fact, I may be less than just to those who defend right, justice, freedom, and the worth of every human being, by believing more, much more, in the power of ideas and in the fact that convictions which unite service to God and to man are irresistible.

When choosing a synthesis of the fundamental rights of man, I instinctively turn to *Pacem in Terris,* an encyclical which was hailed everywhere in the world by Christians and non-Christians, believers and nonbelievers.

To begin with, Pope John reminds us:

In a properly constituted and effective human society, it is a fundamental principle that every human being is a person; that is, a nature endowed with intelligence and free will. For this reason he is possessed of rights and duties emanating directly and simultaneously from his very nature. These rights, therefore, are universal, inviolable, and inalienable.

And if we contemplate the dignity of the human person in the light of revealed truth, we must only hold it in incomparably greater esteem. For we are speaking of human beings redeemed by the Blood of Christ, who by the Grace of God are children and friends of God, the heirs of eternal glory.

We might very well content ourselves with this introduction. Without incriminating anyone in particular, and recognizing that we are speaking of collective sin for which we Christians bear special responsibility, let us be brave enough to admit that in our own Northeast there are millions of fellow creatures who are far from being treated like human beings and children of God.

The landowner thinks it is his right to pay what he wants, when he wants to. Hasn't he already done his workers the huge favor of supplying land and a house and work, and letting them farm their little piece of ground?

If the farm worker wakes up one morning feeling ungrateful and begins thinking he's as good as anybody, getting involved with new things, going to school by radio, joining a union, talking about his rights, the boss is sure he has good reason to be alarmed; he feels the hot breath of subversion, maybe even of Communism, blowing in the wind. And so, without the slightest hesitation or the least remorse, he puts the worker off his land, even if he has to burn down the shack he lives in with his family in order to do it.

He never suspects that in so doing he is violating several of the fundamental rights mentioned by Pope John: the right to life and a decent standard of living; inherent economic rights, especially the right to humane work (healthful, full of decent feeling, free, adequately paid, and with a possibility of acquiring private property); the right to participate in the treasures of culture, and therefore the right to a basic education (a minimal part of those rights concerned with moral and cultural values); the right of meeting and association; the right to worship God according to the dictates of an upright conscience. And if the worker is treated unjustly by someone who believes in God the Father and Creator, and if the worker discovers connivance in this injustice on the part of a Church which is always repeating that we are all brothers, children of the same Heavenly Father, how can that indignant man find the interior serenity and peace of mind to praise God?

It is futile to say that the worker, struggling with his awakening consciousness, will become politicized (a term which for many is a synonym for turning Communist). Among the basic rights of man Pope John lists those of a political nature. Human beings have the right to participate actively in public life and to make their personal contribution to the well-being of all citizens.

A human being cannot be considered a mere object or passive element in society. On the contrary, he must be upheld as the subject, the foundation, and the end of society.

It is with joy that I mention these truths, now that the so-called Natal Movement is becoming internationally known. With Dom Eugênio Sales and Dom Nivaldo Monte leading the way, this movement was the Brazilian pioneer of radio schools and the organization of farm workers' unions.

The phenomenon of human beings living in subhuman conditions is certainly no monopoly of the Brazilian Northeast. In our own country, the Central Plateau is our rival in adversity and Amazônia surpasses us. And what is true of Brazil is also true of two-thirds of Latin America and two-thirds of the world. So it is not hard to see the error in thinking that the colonial era has come to an end. The worst kind of colonialism, internal colonialism, is still very much with us.

Internal colonialism is the enrichment of some of our fellow countrymen at the expense of other fellow countrymen kept in subhuman conditions.

To rebel against *conscientização,* then, is to try to keep the subhuman masses from becoming people; it is to demand that human beings refrain from using their intelligence, their freedom, and their consciences.

To brand *conscientização* as a Communist plot is to do Communism too great a favor by attributing to it a preoccupation with human beings and their fundamental rights.

A familiar objection comes to mind: it is far easier and quicker to arouse social consciousness than to achieve structural reform. If we know this, and we still awaken people's consciousness, aren't we inviting subversion and Communism?

Those who are indeed playing into the hands of Communism are those who feed the revolt of the masses by trying to keep them in a subhuman state; for today, through radio and television, movies and the press, no matter where a man lives he can keep up with what is happening even in the most distant countries.

Is there anyone who does not know that man today is capable of conquering nature and wresting from her what is necessary (and even more than is necessary) to provide a human standard of living for all of us? Is there anyone who does not know that there is no underproduction but only underconsumption, the offspring of superselfishness?

Will the awakened masses lose patience, then, and rush into the streets? And will a bloodletting inevitably follow?

The only way to stop conniving at maintaining the internal colonialism that crushes millions of human beings, while at the same time avoiding the radicalization that leads to hatred and bloodshed, is to arouse the social consciousness of the ruling elite as well as that of the masses.

Anyone who laughs at this proposal as if it were platonic, or quixotic, is confessing that he does not believe in the power of ideas.

Of course it isn't easy to row against the tide, to overcome obstacles or preach to the deaf (and all of us have perfect hearing when the talk is about our rights, and go deaf suddenly when we're reminded of our obligations). It is a matter of stirring up minds and changing hearts.

What good is it to win out by force, to conquer by fire and sword, when hate engenders only hate, when nothing lasting can be built on a foundation of hate? Our task is much greater, much deeper, more difficult, and more beautiful. Our task is to help human beings to conquer their own selfishness and to comprehend that, out of intelligence if not from a spirit of faith, they should see how they might deal more justly with those who work for them, even if they must rend their own flesh in order to do so. Our task is to persuade the slavocrats of the present day to make the abolition of slavery a reality, to make a decisive contribution, not to some broad philanthropic movement of social welfare, but to an authentic movement of human advancement.

Once in my diocese, a thousand fishermen and their families, who were already poor, were on the point of sliding into a state of utter misery. In the developing Brazilian Northeast, a synthetic rubber plant and a vegetable protein factory, among others, had been installed on the bank of a river. The chemical waste flowing into the stream from these two factories was killing the fish and therefore gravely jeopardizing the already precarious situation of those fishermen.

I arranged a meeting between the managers of the two factories and the distressed fishermen. The managers explained that in about two and a half years their factories would be in a position to recycle the wastes; the fishermen would have to be patient until then. In vain the fishermen cried out that in two and a half years they would be living on the verge of starvation if they were not already dead.

We were face to face with one chapter in the universal balance sheet of investments. Unless I am much mistaken, the golden rule is still the same: invest where profits are highest, quickest, and safest. If that means crushing a few, or many, or numerous human beings, it is regrettable, but, the reasoning goes, that is the inevitable price of progress.

And thus we see that Communism has no monopoly on crushing human beings. Apropos of this subject, another important observation should be made. It is touching to see that the West does not hesitate to sacrifice the finest flower of its youth to fight and die to safeguard the free world.

When will the countries of the West become fully conscious of the fact that misery, too, crushes human beings and reduces them to a vile subhuman state?

When will we fully understand that "freedom" is a word without meaning to someone who does not have a house fit to live in, or food fit to eat, or clothes fit to wear, or a minimum of education and decent work?

It isn't easy to be rich and go on being human. It isn't easy to deprive oneself voluntarily of goods which may not be worth much today but will certainly be worth more tomorrow, or to think of others, or to listen to the Church when she reminds us that the right to property is never absolute and unconditional, or to make up our minds not to keep what is a luxury to us but a necessity to others.

Democracy must come to the aid of human frailty. If it does not lead in bringing about unions of free workers, free cooperatives, and free adult elementary education, there will be a serious lack of these democratic instruments of human advancement and community organization.

Some fear the possible abuses of liberty and foresee all kinds of pressure, threats, violence, a climate of uncertainty and uneasiness, all harbingers of social convulsion.

The government has the right and duty to insist that adult education, unions, and cooperatives be organized within the limits of the law and be restricted to the democratic process. But as long as they act within the law and the democratic process, they should not be subjected to the least constraint, they should be entirely free to act. Otherwise they will turn into caricatures of what they ought to be.

Is there anyone who does not know that on our continent the number of those who no longer believe in democracy and are ready to turn to violence is growing by leaps and bounds, precisely because they judge democracy to be timid and indecisive? They consider it to be without the courage to go to the root of our evils because out of fear it walks with such excessive caution that it ends by being inoperative and useless?

If we love democracy and believe in its methods, we must demand much of it. Democracy has no right to be blind and deaf, no right to be naïve. There are grave wrongs to be righted, above all in the rural areas. Mere pathetic appeals to the heartstrings, laws on paper, and bureaus with pompous names are not enough.

If we are sincere in our desire for human advancement and truly want to organize our communities—the initial step in authentic development—we should be overjoyed to see the workers struggling to get a basic education and running their own unions and their own cooperatives, without constraint or paternalism, without fear and without puppet leaders imposed from above.

So that the calumny of Communist sympathies on my part will not be repeated, this may be a good time to remind you that the selfish attitude of the United States during the first United Nations Conference on Trade and Development—a conference of vital importance to the underdeveloped world—was equaled only by that of Soviet Russia. So that it will not be alleged that my attitude is anti-American, let me point out one example, among many, in which we might profitably imitate the United States: it would be greatly to our advantage to adopt an antitrust law like that adopted, for domestic use, by the North Americans.

This is a good time to remind the three branches of government of this Republic, a good time to remind this democracy of Brazil, that they must urgently seek ways and means of enforcing the laws passed by the legislature and promulgated by the executive branch. It is perilous in the extreme, it is an evil of unforeseeable consequences, to allow the laws to be discredited.

It grieves me to see that not only in Brazil, but to a greater or lesser degree in all of Latin America, many of the best of our young people find it harder and harder to trust in democracy; to have faith in its validity, in its forthrightness in moving from theory to practice, in its courage to go straight to the heart of our socioeconomic ills and find a remedy for them.

Time is running out against democracy. Greater and greater numbers have become disenchanted with it and are in danger of falling either into a skeptical, even cynical attitude or into one of violence and despair.

It would be a grave error to take the scornful, superior stand of one who trusts public authority to break up any manifestations of violence. The solution this country needs is quite different: it is that the government and the people, the nation's vital forces, in a common love of freedom and democracy, join forces to transform fundamental laws which have heretofore existed only on paper into living laws for a living people who have a rendezvous with their own destiny.

Surely it is not so hard to sense the love concealed behind slogans which may sometimes sound harsh to the ear. If we cling too tightly to our rings, we must remember that we are in danger of losing not only our fingers but our arms. If I demand much of democracy, it is because I believe in it. And it grieves me to see the democracies losing ground because their rich are getting richer and their poor are getting poorer.

My harshness toward certain countries may be a quixotic effort—but who does not love and respect Don Quixote, who is so much more a realist than he seems, very much worth listening to by politicians who call themselves practical and yet topple over into the most incredible lack of realism? My harshness toward certain countries, I repeat, is what may be a quixotic effort to help them understand that in the middle run, for I cannot say in the long run, it is suicidal to persist in widening the growing gulf between the developed and the developing worlds.

5

The Role of Youth

Some words are watersheds, symbols of controversy. I am thinking of one of those words today, not because I want to irritate anyone, to wound or provoke, but because I am convinced that it corresponds to an attitude that is an urgent necessity for any country aspiring to be democratic in more than name. This word, this idea, is *dialogue*.

If the whole country is in need of dialogue, if even children must be initiated in the art of dialogue, if dialogue is essential even for those who never reach primary school, just think how necessary to a university is an atmosphere favorable to dialogue.

Dialogue isn't easy; we all know that. Sometimes we even have difficulty carrying on a dialogue with ourselves, so great are the internal contradictions of anyone who can and does say, with St. Paul:

> *For I do not the good that I wish, but the evil that I do not wish, that I perform.*

If it has always been difficult for old and young to understand one another, think of what is happening now, when ten years might as well be a hundred and when, in the past quarter of a century, man has made more numerous and more bewildering discoveries than in all the preceding millennia of human history.

The adult who does not know how to grow old gracefully, who does not keep his mind young and open to every moment's innovations, is bound to suffer terribly and to clash head on with the young.

There are parents who are unable to free themselves from the authoritarianism in which they were brought up (some of them still remember a time when married sons did not dare light a cigarette in their father's presence). There are parents who would think they were losing their authority if they talked to young people as one adult to another, without accentuating the distance between educator and pupil. There are parents who are not at all open to the psychology of the young, who are not at all inclined to have faith in them, who are unwilling to treat their children more as a friend than as a stern paterfamilias.

Such fathers would think it a preposterous breach of discipline to have to give their children reasons for their actions. The worst of it is that sometimes all this show of authority is not backed up by anything solid and the children discover, without too much effort, that the moralistic façade is full of deplorable cracks.

Of course, it is not always easy to hold a dialogue with young people. Frequently they lack the slightest inclination to accept a different way of thinking on the part of their parents; their criticisms are merciless and excessive; they want to be treated like adults but act in irresponsible and childish ways; they insist on having their own way, which is not infrequently extravagant and capricious.

Similar difficulties might easily be listed when it comes to the relationship between teachers and students. It is easy to demand that the schools have high standards; that research be conducted in every department; that lectures not be repeated year after year and that crib sheets become a thing of the past; that spontaneous, natural communication flow from one department to another; that every school be in touch with the others, and that all make an effort to become a relevant part of their environment.

It should be obvious that not all of the young people who

demand so much of their college or university are models of what a student should be. Sometimes they make no effort to learn. They thoughtlessly take advantage of university politics but have no foundation on which to construct something a little more solid.

Good will must be nourished from both sides. If adults, especially parents and professors, throw themselves heart and soul into the work of bravely re-examining their own authority, young people will be much more likely to examine the defects and exaggerations in their own freedom. If home and school show enough good will to re-examine their excessive prudence, traditionalism, and order, it will be easier for the young to re-examine their excessive rashness, innovativeness, and lack of order.

When no one will give an inch, when all are adamant, the tension soon becomes intolerable. Since education can take place only insofar as the person educated consents to be taught, and eventually to teach himself, an atmosphere of cold war and mutual ill will makes the work of serious education all but impossible.

An example of internal disarmament toward the young should come from the official education authorities. The war between young people and the Ministry of Education must not be allowed to continue, for if it does not stop, the Ministry will push more and more youths over the line into clandestine radicalism.

There are very serious and weighty problems to be considered: young people are in the ascendancy all over the world; Latin America is the continent of the young, in the light of official statistics which register the well-known but still startling numerical preponderance of young people in the population. In Brazil only a tiny proportion of our children reach the universities. Ministry of Education statistics show that many never even reach primary school and more never finish, while an ever-dwindling number of lucky ones reach junior high, high school, and go on to higher education. . . .

The logic seems inescapable: we must conclude that Brazilian universities have not only the right but the obligation to take an interest in the great problems of their region, their country, their continent, and the world.

Our government recognizes a citizen's obligation to vote at the age of eighteen. How can a young university student be expected to vote conscientiously or rationally if he is forbidden to examine and discuss the grave problems of the present day?

We all recognize the urgency of national economic integration. Surely no one can be so wrongheaded as to want the university to stand aloof from the effort to integrate whole areas of our territory and whole groups of our population. It should be obvious, rather, that the university can be a natural leader, and, in fact, that the university should obviously take a leading role in this blessed struggle which is so vital to our country's welfare and such a fundamental part of the contribution which we are in all conscience obliged to make in the attempt to integrate Latin America into a whole.

Unfortunately, the lack of dialogue between individuals leads to a lack of dialogue between groups and eventually to a lack of dialogue between peoples and nations.

However far man may advance in science and technical knowledge, as long as there are wars in the world we will be bearing dismal witness to our lack of spiritual maturity. As long as the proof of a party's rightness is seen to lie in its superior power of destruction, all of us who call ourselves educators must recognize that we have failed. Religions, educational systems, and families will lose much of their moral strength because we shall have been helpless to prevent two world wars in a century and powerless to check the arms race which is a permanent threat to man's very presence on the face of the earth.

It is true that our century did produce the United Nations, an attempt at dialogue on a global scale.

Out of love for humanity; out of love for that world peace which has been imperiled by two world wars and innumerable local conflicts; out of respect and love for the UN itself, which had the honor of being visited by the greatest spiritual leader of our time, Pope Paul VI, we must find the courage to ask what the UN must do to free the world from ignominious affronts to dialogue like the Wall of Shame in Berlin and the Iron Curtain that closes a large part of humanity off from normal human companionship; what it must do to effectively overcome the terrible list of raging or potential conflicts—Vietnam in the lead—which rendered virtually helpless a capable leader like Secretary-General U Thant.

Unless I am very much mistaken, there are two gestures that would give immense and immediate moral reinforcement to the United Nations, which already has a fine record of service to humanity:

1. The UN should end the veto privilege enjoyed by the so-called Big Four (for all practical purposes Soviet Russia and the United States). It is a curious assembly of peers in which a very few enjoy power which is unequal and clearly stands in the way of world dialogue.

2. The UN should make up its mind to run the risk of admitting Mainland China as a member, out of conviction that its claim to represent the world is gravely impaired when such a large slice of humanity is excluded from the right to dialogue within the United Nations.

Recently, when China was once again refused membership, a delegate remarked: "Admitting China would be like letting a tiger into the cage with us." I understand his point. But we should ask ourselves this: what would have become of the Gubbian wolf without the love and understanding of St. Francis of Assisi?

In a Nazi concentration camp—and the same thing might well have happened in a Communist concentration camp—there was found an instrument of torture, a whip, on which was mockingly inscribed the word "dialogue." And the word which totalitarians of all names and stripes misunderstand, reject, and ridicule should be a sacred heritage to youth. Young people should form a constituency, should be apostles of dialogue, in the heart of our society which has so little patience to listen. They, like the rest of us, should learn how to hear; learn to respect thoughts that differ from their own.

There would be little hope for us if we met only praise and approval along our path: we might start to believe the good things we heard about ourselves, and that is usually the beginning of the end.

Opposition is uncomfortable, even painful. Nevertheless, it is always preferable to flattery. If we never encounter obstacles in our way, we are apt to go farther than we meant to.

Dialogue helps us take our own measure. It keeps us from withdrawing into the shell of our own egos. It opens us to our neighbor and to God.

There are some who think that Brazilian youth lacks moral fibre and dedication. You can tell they have not carried on a dialogue with the young. Those very same long-haired kids are longing for the university to play an effective role in the reality of contemporary Brazil. Of course they reject entirely that worst form of "cooption," the naming by outsiders of young people to lead the youth movement. Leaders cannot be imposed from outside, they arise from within. Of course the atmosphere will not be right for young people as long as there is a climate of fear. Which is better, healthier, more democratic, more constructive, more honest, more human: being afraid that the young may think, preventing them from talking, radicalizing them and pushing them into clandestine activities, or accepting an occasional, inevitable overexuberance of language and attitude, which contains its built-in safeguard—the great desire of the young to help build, and a deep and genuine thirst to assert themselves?

It has been said that students ought to study, and that if they were really studying seriously they would have no time left to agitate. Well, put reality on the curriculum; include something about the pressing problems of this region, this country, this continent, and the world, and the young will study. Incidentally, let's not delude ourselves: they *do* study. They are far better informed about national and international problems than adults suppose.

Young people, those identical youths who baffle their elders with rock music and record players going full blast and filling the whole building with their racket, want, in fact demand, something better than a university that's nothing but a high school with a fancy name; they demand professors who don't settle into a dull routine and stagnate; they demand above all a university that is the true propellant force of national integration.

Let's open a brave and unlimited credit account to our young people before it's too late. Halfhearted confidence in them will never satisfy the young. After all, my fellow adults, are these young people your children or aren't they? Are you forgetting that the young have always shared our national and international concerns? We have only to ask ourselves whether Brazil would have abolished slavery or become a republic when it did if it had not been for the courageous participation of our youth.

Excesses? It's normal for them to crop up here and there. The day our youth is as temperate, cautious, and coolheaded as old age, the country will perish of boredom.

Felipe Herrera, President of the Inter-American Development Bank and a man whose authority cannot be denied, said in a recent document on the role of the universities in Latin-American development:

We can hardly expect the universities not to reflect the terrible problems and critical circumstances shaping the reality of our developing region. The difficulties and tensions which derive from an overall situation characterized by an insufficient economic development incapable of coping with growing demographic pressures; an unjust distribution of wealth that clashes with the yearning for a better life on the part of large masses of the people; the exodus of rural populations to the cities and the fact that our fledgling industries are incapable of absorbing this uprooted work force; the formation, despite all these adverse factors, of a new middle class, which demands new opportunities and with them new responsibilities; and the influence of the global ideological struggle are some of the realities inevitably reflected in our universities. The preoccupations of our political and intellectual leaders will inevitably have repercussions in the universities and in student attitudes, especially when those leaders proclaim the urgency of our continent's need to progress, and the necessity for this progress to come at once, reforming or radically transforming decrepit, outdated structures in its precipitous course. It would be strange, unheard-of, alarming, indeed, were this not so. In countries undergoing such an intensive process of transformation, a quiet, passive university makes no sense at all; it might even hold the society back.

Of course Felipe Herrera distinguishes the natural restlessness of youth, the understandable and desirable preoccupation of the young with national and world problems, from the professional agitation of those who infiltrate the student milieu solely in order to upset the prevailing system, sow hatred, and foment chaos. However, the astute Herrera sounds this timely alert:

Not infrequently an "ism" is attached to what is actually nothing more than an expression of our young people's dissatisfaction at the university's failure to furnish the sort of solution they are looking for to the great problems they are distressed to see around them.

While admitting that this dissatisfaction is dangerous when carried to extremes, Herrera reminds us that conformity, especially in our young societies, constitutes "another kind of fatalistic colonialism, the bondage of one resigned to his fate who expects help to come from the outside."

Unless I am much mistaken, university students today, particularly, perhaps, those of Latin America, are increasingly confronted with two fundamental options: Christianity and Marxism.

Anyone who thinks that Christianity is outdated and no longer appeals to intelligent young people on the threshold of the twenty-first century is deceiving himself. Presently I will cite various reasons why Christianity is regaining the respect and sympathy even of non-Christians, agnostics, and atheists.

As for Marxism, it is futile to treat it simplistically or imagine that it can be swept from the university milieu by force. We should not deceive ourselves. It has been said, and rightly, that Marxism is basically humanistic: its aim is to elevate mankind to the highest degree of self-fulfillment. It would banish whatever dehumanizes or alienates man, the better to release the vast innate possibilities latent in him.

When we see how seriously Christianity and Marxism measure and confront each other in our day—each recognizing the differences and knowing they are rivals, yet respecting the other; one calling itself "the methodology of the historical initiative toward fulfillment of the whole man" while the other prefers to be "the theology of the absolute future"—we can better understand why the youth of today, which has so much more depth and seriousness than many people think, is torn between the two most appealing *isms* of contemporary life.

The present feeling of good will toward religion began, unless I am wrong, as a consequence of the ecumenical attitude assumed by the Church of Vatican II. Young people are pleased to see that Catholics, while not forgetting their serious differences with Protestants, are concentrating on Christ, in whom Catholics and Protestants are joined in brotherhood. Young people are pleased at the new way in which the Catholic Church speaks of Jews: instead of insisting on calling them traitors, in the sense of having betrayed the faith, we now have enough humility to recall that every one of us is constantly exposed to the danger of betraying his faith. And instead of throwing the spotlight on what separates us from the Jews, we are glad to recall that the God we invoke is the God of Abraham, Isaac, and Jacob; that it is David's psalms we sing; that Christ, as a man, was Jewish and so was Our Lady, Mother of God and Mother of Men.

Our young people are also favorably impressed by the Church's new openness toward non-Christian religions; its firm and honest attitude toward religious freedom, and its broad-minded understanding of agnostics and atheists, and even of those who persecute it.

Good will toward religion is broadening as the university students become familiar with the position of the Church on such matters as the following:

• Christianity does not shrink back in fear and trembling at man's audacity in splitting the atom, surpassing the wildest dreams of the alchemists, flinging stars into the heavens, preparing to voyage into outer space and embark on still greater and more dizzying feats. Christianity exults at seeing man obey the Divine command to have dominion over nature and finish the work of Creation.

• Christianity is not attached to any one economic, social, or political system: it calls for the safeguarding of the common good and the practice of justice and charity. More specifically, Christianity has no commitment to capitalism or to the economic and social structures which in many cases do not favor the participation and integration of the great masses into society but leave them stranded and alienated from its commercial, political, social, and cultural institutions.

• Christianity, while safeguarding the natural right to private property, feels it necessary to affirm that the basic right of all to the use of material goods comes before private property, and that it is necessary to act firmly and wisely to counter the accumulation of property in the hands of a few.

• Christianity is distressed to see that the gap between the developed and the underdeveloped worlds, far from diminishing, is regrettably, horribly, increasing; dismayed to see the decade of development announced by the UN for 1960–1970 drawing to a melancholy close, and grieved to note that the situation can only worsen as long as the rich countries see their relations with the underdeveloped countries in terms of aid, when the problem is one of justice on a world-wide scale.

• Christianity is aware that without justice there can be no peace among men. But we have no faith in armed battles. We want war abolished, as the shame and opprobrium to the human species that it is. When will we stop being such savages as to imagine that the proof of a people's superiority consists in crushing others? How long will we keep up the absurdity and the cannibalism of war, well aware that our power of destruction has been so far perfected that both sides own sufficient force to wipe human life from the face of the earth? How long will we keep up our stupid games of wars, hot and cold, when humanity is aware that we have the knowledge and technical resources to face any population explosion that may lie ahead? Only one explosion is really fatal: that of selfishness.

The university students go along with us this far. Even when certain of their statements seem radical and excessive to adults, the young people understand, applaud, and demand only that we be consistent enough to practice what we preach.

It is precisely at this point that some of them lose faith in the Church, judging that it lacks the moral fiber to put its theories into practice and the skill to state its theories in a clear, firm, coherent manner. It is here that many turn to Marxism.

Enlightened Marxists no longer simply repeat that religion is the opiate of the people. Rounding out Marxist thought with quotations from Marx himself, they recognize that while Christianity is an expression of a wretched reality, it is also a protest against that reality.

The Marxists test the Christians by distinguishing in each historical era between reflex and protest, opiate and illuminating guide, faith and ideology, the hour of Constantine and that of the Apocalypse, fundamental demand and alienation.

We must make the Marxists know, feel, and see that if we Christians do not arm for battle or wage guerrilla warfare it is not for lack of courage. It is because the Gospel is much more demanding, much more revolutionary than Marx.

What good will it do to replace men and governments if the same old mentality prevails? We must break down the structures in people's minds, stir up their consciences, engage their wills. If we fail to do that, no amount of intelligence and devotion to agrarian-development bureaus, for example, will be enough: agrarian reform will be words written on paper; internal colonialism will prevail, and so will the vegetative, subhuman existence of millions of Brazilians, even more millions of Latin Americans, and still more millions of human beings throughout the Third World.

To young people who thirst for plain speaking we shall have to explain how we intend to go beyond our naïve assumptions, our sentimental sermonizing and ineffectual appeals, even though we seem to lack what they see as the courage of absolute conviction, the decision to make up our minds once and for all to join those who are revolutionary in deed as well as word.

It so happens that we believe in the power of ideas. As long as only a few bishops, priests, or laymen spoke out and acted upon the social teachings of the Church, particularly Vatican II, it was easy to brand them as Communist subversives. But now that is beginning to change. The purpose of our meeting of Latin-American bishops in Mar del Plata was to examine, at the express wish of Pope Paul VI, how we might best involve the Church in the development and integration of Latin America.

It was rumored that we bishops had quarreled among ourselves; that the conservatives had blocked the way to any daring idea; that the meeting had been a resounding failure.

Not so. The agreement among the bishops was impressive. The conclusions we reached, with the help of topnotch technicians, are both valid and bold. And they have the full approval of the Holy Father.

Our theology of development begins with a theology of

Creation, embraces Christian anthropology, and arrives at an ethic of development. We have a whole body of principles which do not stop at generalities: they are practical and concrete.

Anyone who wants to think that the reason I spend so much time at the universities talking to young people is that I have plenty of time to kill or an irresistible urge to show off, is free to do so.

Even with the help of our priests and laymen, even if we bend all our skills to cooperating and working together, the bishops of Brazil and even of all Latin America can never by ourselves topple the outmoded economic, social, and cultural structures of this continent.

But if the Brazilian universities unfurl the banner of national integration, other universities on the continent will join the march toward the development and integration of Latin America.

My Young Friends:

Thanks be to God, in every place and every time young people have imagined and will imagine, yesterday, today, and forevermore, that they are different and that it is up to them to build a better world.

But in a special sense I believe that your youth coincides, in a marvelous way, with the triple youth of Brazil, our continent, and the world.

It would be a terrible thing to come too late into a world in which nothing remains to be done. But that can happen only to the unfortunate without creative imagination or eyes to perceive.

This is an exciting time to be living in Brazil, now that we have the task of awakening and conquering Amazônia; but we shall be unworthy of that task unless our conquest of Amazônia is for Brazil and for the world, for men and for God.

It is exciting to have the Central Plateau and the Northeast to develop; exciting to make the ideals of freedom which we celebrate on September 7 and May 13 a reality; exciting to undertake the work of national integration and to find our own best solutions to our country's problems.

You are very lucky that national dimensions are not enough: the integration of the continent, too, must be tackled without delay.

Dialogue between the very strong and the very weak is meaningless. If we are to be in a position to carry on a dialogue with the rest of the world, we must, in our devotion to the idea of universal unity:

- Forget our illusions about alliances which end up as a form of aid by the underdeveloped countries to the superpowers.
- Be realistic enough and humble enough to know that if any of our countries is to emerge from underdevelopment, we must share our resources and support one another on this continent.
- Take the glorious risk of refusing tutelage from anyone.
- Avoid subjecting our smaller neighbors to the same kind of hegemony and imperialism which we are learning to oppose for ourselves.

But even our continent is too small a world for you: think always in terms of the Third World. When will we begin to pay our debt to Africa? (For three centuries the Americas enslaved millions of Africans!) When will we really understand that we all have the obligation to be brothers to Asia, for it is there that the definitive battle for development will be won or lost?

Time is running against us. But in the accelerated march of history, it is your generation which must see that the Third World is seated, not as a beggar, but as a brother and an equal, at the table which is round at last, fitted for the dialogue among all the nations of the world.

The earth itself is too small for you. Don't limit yourselves to the dimensions of one planet. You are going to land on the stars. You will live to see the end of the arms race and the end of war, not because of idealistic motives but for very realistic ones: war has become impracticable, absurd.

You will humanize the electronic and cybernetic age. You will escape the robots and attain the true socialization, at the service of man and the community, dreamed of by Pope John.

Do not be surprised that I am not astonished at what I am telling you: the youth of Brazil and the world corresponds to a new and youthful Christianity.

The post-Vatican II Christian is a man without fear. He knows that ever since the supreme moment when human life came into being, our Creator and Father has trusted man with the responsibility of carrying on the work of evolution. He is happy to see that after centuries of feeling like a child, man is now beginning to believe in his right and duty to have dominion over nature and finish the work of Creation; he is beginning to take command of history.

If it is true that the shadow of sin introduced fear, weakness, and death into the land of men, it is no less true that Christ came to live in anticipation of the plenitude that men will reach with the help of Grace. Christ appeared because it will take superhuman effort to humanize the subhumans created by misery and the supermen dehumanized by too much comfort.

He came so that men will not fall into temptation when their own discoveries lead them to think themselves more than stewards, able to dispense with God.

Christ is the answer to our irresistible calling to be gods, a longing which is far from ridiculous pretension or empty dream. We were born to be gods. And in our encounter with Christ as He really is—not deformed, caricatured, unrecognizable— we are plunged directly into Divine Life.

Not long ago there were those who wanted to forbid you the right to sing the Brazilian national anthem and display the Brazilian flag in the International Theater Festival. But it so happens that Brazil belongs to you. More than that: you are Brazil.

It's true that you protest, complain, demand. But how can you be denied the right to demand, complain, protest, when you were brought to life without being consulted about it, tossed into this unjust, war-torn world of ours?

All we can ask in our fraternal dialogue with you is that your protest be more and more a constructive one, as it was when you showed the world what you could do in *Morte e Vida Severina,* that drama of life and death in the Brazilian Northeast.

The most we can ask in this fraternal dialogue (clergy without clericalism, parents without paternalism) is that when you give us your extraordinary lesson in open-mindedness and humanism, you show a little bit of patience with those who were born and brought up in an atmosphere of narrowness and egotism.

Have you noticed how boldly I speak in this letter to you, as if I were one of you?

Youth is no more the lack of wrinkles and white hair than old age is the mere having lived for a long time. You know that being young means having a cause to dedicate your life to. And *we* have a triple cause to fill our lives to overflowing: as Brazilians, to live the youth of Brazil; as men, to live the youth of the world; as Christians (and remember, Christ is no one's private property, He came to save us all), to live the eternal youth of Christ.

6

Relations Between Two Worlds

That man is both great and frail is a truth that each of us can prove to himself at every instant; that man is both mighty and absurdly weak can be verified by simply opening our eyes and looking at the world around us.

In our personal lives we see the best intentions, the most ambitious plans, the most determined vows broken, often on the very day they are made, as we do the very opposite of what we promised ourselves or others.

And when we look clearly at the human cavalcade, we discover:

• That man has the intelligence, genius, skill, and perseverance to split the atom but did not hesitate to make his initial use of atomic energy that of razing two cities to the ground and leaving the few survivors with a heritage of external and internal mutilation that was worse than instant death.

• That man is a demigod capable of sowing stars, who has already launched more than one hundred satellites around the earth and moon, but who builds walls of shame and curtains of iron, and who carries on racial struggles like that of the whites against the blacks in the United States and the blacks against the whites in South Africa.

• That man is swiftly preparing to venture into space—tomorrow to the moon, then to the planets and beyond, in a leap from galaxy to galaxy; but that even after the horror of two world wars in a single generation he is still powerless to put a stop to local wars, including the wretched, shameful conflict in Vietnam.

• That what man is able to extract from petroleum is astounding, the world of electronics is like science fiction, and the consequences of automation are unforeseeable but certainly revolutionary; yet the tragic truth is that year by year the gap separating the developed and the underdeveloped worlds yawns wider and deeper.

It is worthwhile stopping here for a moment to take a look at a few vignettes of our dangerous human folly. According to official UN statistics:

• Forty million Asians, Africans, and Latin Americans starve to death each year. The United Nations was horrified to learn this, and it was agreed that every developed country would make an annual contribution of one percent of its respective gross national product to reduce the slaughter. One percent! Well, not even this drop in the bucket has ever been achieved: in 1961 the developed countries contributed 0.87 percent, and by 1964 the percentage had fallen to 0.66 percent.

• In Europe there is a doctor for every thousand inhabitants; in Ghana, one for every eighteen thousand; in Indonesia, one for every seventy-one thousand; in the Sudan, one for every eighty thousand.

• In Brazil a child dies every 42 seconds; 85 die every hour; 2,040 children every day.

It would be only too easy to keep piling up this kind of statistic to confirm in the most painful way that man's greatness is comparable only to his madness (and his lack of balance), for numbers like these reveal that there is something profoundly wrong in the relations among men.

And yet it has never been so exciting to be human. There was a time when man felt himself to be so helpless, so unarmed before nature that he believed in a blind, cruel fate more powerful than the gods themselves. Today man is so much in command of nature that he no longer thinks of himself as a plaything of occult and omnipotent forces; he considers himself as acting upon history and controlling events, the master of his fate. To his great surprise, religion itself meets him halfway and reminds him that his attitude is in no way an affront or an offense against God, Who chose to make man in His own image and ordered him to have dominion over nature and to complete the work of Creation.

There are in the world 150 million people suffering from malaria, and man has discovered the specific drug which can save his 150 million brothers. He even knows exactly how much it would cost to save them: $1.6 billion.

There are in the world 250 million children without schools, and man not only knows how to do away with illiteracy by using audio-visual resources, establishing radiophonic schools, teaching by television, but he has the available experience and technical resources to bring about the full self-awareness of the masses through basic education and popular culture.

There are two hundred million workers in the world who lose one hundred working days each year (twenty billion days lost!), yet man has mastered machines to the point where they can do the work of millions.

There are doomsayers who cry out that the world's present three billion inhabitants will be 6.5 billion by the year 2000. But even without counting the Arabian Nights riches prophesied to lie at the end of future space trips, even without tapping the wealth lying at the bottom of the sea, agriculture, of which chemistry is now the handmaiden, keeps us from worrying about those numbers. When one thinks of the expansion of arable land; when one keeps in mind the war on pests, the selective improvement of seeds and all that irrigation can accomplish, then the neo-Malthusians' lack of creative imagination becomes patently evident, along with much that is hypocritical and suspect in the massive birth-control campaigns directed from outside our shores.

It is understandable that Europe should be in a panic at the thought that by the famous year 2000 it will have only 10 percent of the world's population; equally understandable the alarm of the United States when it is reminded that by then it will not only have a mere 5 percent of the earth's inhabitants, but in its population there will be a strong preponderance of blacks to boot—the same blacks who so horrify the segregationists of the South.

China will have 1.5 billion inhabitants, the equivalent of the entire population of the earth in 1900. China and India together will have 2.5 billion people, almost as many as the present population of the world.

It must be intolerably dull to begin living and then find all the problems solved and the house straightened up, with almost nothing left to do. It must be tragic to feel impotent in the face of insoluble problems. What is fascinating is to confront grave, very grave problems and yet be aware that solutions are within our reach, dependent only on our good judgment and our ability to overcome our own selfishness.

We must find a way to free humanity from two forms of madness that complement and aggravate each other: the madness of war and the madness that leads to the continual widening of the gulf between the developed and the underdeveloped worlds.

Every day war becomes a greater absurdity. Let us now take to heart the words of Arnold Toynbee:

The atomic bomb has changed the nature of war. In the past, we could say that a soldier fought on the battlefront, risked his life and often sacrificed it to save his family, his native land, his own kind. When Leonidas' 300 offered their lives at Thermopylae, they knew that in that rocky pass they were saving Sparta.

Today this is no longer true. If the Spartans had known that the chief of Xerxes' military command was able, by pressing a button in far-off Asia Minor, to destroy all of them at once—and not only them, but their wives, their children, and their fellow citizens—the situation would have been profoundly different.

The reasons which induce a soldier to offer his life have disappeared. In the past, it was better to win than to lose. The victor received land, dominions, rewards, honor, and deference. The atomic bomb has seen to it that the distinction between winner and loser is destroyed.

Let us listen to an even more compelling voice: that of Pope Paul VI at the UN, exclaiming in unforgettable tones:

Never war, war never again! The moment has come for conversion, for personal rebirth, for inner renewal. We must become accustomed to looking at man in a new way: in a new way at our life in common; in a new way, in short, at the paths of history and the fate of the world. Never more than today, in an age marked by such great human progress, has it been more necessary to appeal to the moral conscience of man. For the danger comes not from progress or science, which, used wisely, can solve many of the grave problems assailing humanity. The real danger is deep-rooted in man, who has at his disposal ever more powerful instruments, as well adapted to ruin as to the highest victories.

Twin sister to the madness of war is the madness that tends to make more shocking the distance between the developed and the underdeveloped worlds.

Let who will delude himself: the Church has taken Feltin's phrase, "Development is the new name for peace," and made it her own.

Who is unaware that there can be no peace without justice, and that it is justice—nothing more and nothing less than *justice*—that is lacking in the relations between the wealthy nations and the Third World?

Until the nineteenth century, at least, and during the three centuries that preceded it, we reduced 200 million Africans to slavery, deported tens of millions of these, and brought about the deaths of as many other Negroes, our brothers.

Then came the colonialist experiment, and the delusion of the "civilizing mission," which induced even missionaries to cover the military conquerors with a cloak of morality.

Superficially it may seem that the days of slavery are gone, but in Latin America slaves still exist under other names, kept in subhuman conditions by fellow countrymen who will not hear of changing the present unjust and fettering socioeconomic structures.

We say that colonialism is dead, but Latin America, after a century and a half of experience, can inform Asia and Africa that political independence without economic independence is an empty word.

In Western Europe, each country has set aside its own limited individual interests to embrace wider continental interests. All humanity must, at last, proscribe wars as ridiculous and underdevelopment as unworthy of man on the threshold of the twenty-first century.

In sum, what must we do in order to exercise the profession of being human? Does experience not teach us that frailty is our sister, so that however many marvels we achieve, selfishness will always be with us, like a worm in the fruit of our noblest intentions and our purest ideals?

It is all too easy to sink into fatalism and persuade ourselves that there is no hope for us. But surely man will not give up the struggle to master himself just when he has finally achieved mastery over nature.

True strength, in fact, is not a matter of weight lifting or ordering other people around. What good would a Batman be who could do nothing for himself? What good would it do a leader to move multitudes and manipulate them as he pleased if he had no control over himself?

Selfishness, that is the enemy and the source of unhappiness. Individual selfishness, family selfishness, regional selfishness, national selfishness, continental selfishness, international selfishness.

Man has come to the most dramatic crossroads of his history: he is just as capable of conquering misery and ensuring to all humanity a standard of living compatible with human dignity as he is capable of destroying the world and human life. If selfishness wins out, we plunge into chaos. If selfishness is conquered and left behind, we will achieve the harmonious civilization which the great Father Lebret dreamed of all his life.

The best path to take to overcome our selfishness is to draw closer to Christ. Not a Christ deformed by our frailty as Christians, but Christ in His true dimensions, as the Gospel shows Him and as He is seen emerging from the Ecumenical Council, Vatican II. He alone can free man from his egoism and slake his thirst for the Divine. He alone can help humanity fulfill itself, as foreseen in the plans of Our Creator and Father.

When the United States calls upon its youth to fight and, if necessary, to die in defense of the free world:

- To what extent is this appeal based on an objective view of reality?
- To what extent are other reasons joined to the supposed defense of the free world, and in what measure are those reasons valid?
- By doing what they feel to be in their own best interests, to what extent do North Americans place all humanity in danger of extermination?

Let us consider these questions one by one.

Do fighting and dying for the free world correspond to an objective vision of reality? Unless I am mistaken, the United States acts on the assumption that Communism is the supreme evil. No sacrifice is too great to keep the Communists from crushing human beings, suppressing freedom, breaking up families, destroying religion, and trying to uproot the very idea of God. Hence so much money spent and so many lives lost, yesterday in Korea, today in Vietnam, and tomorrow wherever they must.

But why don't the North American universities listen, now, to Peace Corps Volunteers back from tours in Africa, Latin America, and Asia? Why not let them describe the conditions in which two-thirds of humanity are living? Why not ask them to describe what subhuman living conditions are? North Ameri-

can professors and university students would then be convinced
that misery crushes human beings to such an extent that it is
simply not possible to include the two-thirds of the human race
who vegetate in a subhuman state as part of the free world.

If their state is not human, that means that intelligence and
freedom cannot function. It is a world of slaves, not of free men.
Even if their state is politically independent, even if slavery has
been officially abolished, it is still a slave state.

It is not enough to argue that the United States is also combating misery by sending tons of food, clothes, and medicine
wherever there is hunger. We will see in due time that the problem is not one of aid.

For now we will simply take note of the error of including
regions of misery in the free world.

Are there other reasons besides that of the so-called defense
of the so-called free world? We have a duty to be honest with
ourselves and honest with the young people we are sending
off to kill and be killed: is it truly human freedom we are defending, or is it a struggle to safeguard the neo-capitalist world
that the United States embodies and represents?

Today the United States and the Soviet Union are much
closer to one another than is conceivable to the ingenuous anti-
Communists who tremble with horror before the hammer and
sickle. No one who can see his hand in front of his face should
be surprised if the United States and the Soviet Union band together to confront China.

To what extent is the pretext of combating alien ideologies
really a collision of interests, the clash of empires?

In this clash and this collision, each side rivals the other in
atrocities. Just as the United Nations, from time to time, sends
observers to the battlefields, why don't the North American
universities send observers to the Vietnam front to investigate
whether U.S. bombers, in the name of defending liberty and
the dignity of human beings, are razing open cities, committing
nameless atrocities against women and children, sowing death
and destruction?

And so that the United States will not be tempted to set off an atomic war, now is the time when we must investigate the truth of the rumor that, faced with an impasse which is costing more in money and human lives than World War II, the United States has already set up launching pads for nuclear bombs against Vietnam.

If the rumor is false, we can all breathe easier. But it is unthinkable to risk the barbarous re-enactment of another Hiroshima and Nagasaki.

I believe it is urgent to start a dialogue between European and North American universities on the one side and those of Latin America, Africa, and Asia on the other, so that together they can try to work for world peace.

To this end it would be an excellent thing to examine the question of whether or not the relations between the developed and the underdeveloped worlds are out of kilter.

The developing world cries out that when a comparison is made between the money invested in the underdeveloped world by the industrialized countries and the money they get back, and, above all, when we compare the aid received by the underdeveloped world with the losses it suffers as a consequence of the low prices imposed on its raw materials, we find that there is indeed injustice on a global scale.

It is not a question, then, of saying that the aid offered by the United Nations for the development of the poor countries is insufficient. It is true that one percent of the gross national product is a drop in the bucket; it is true that the United Nations have not even achieved that one percent, and it is also true that such figures seem even more ridiculous and meaningless when compared to the sums that are spent on war.

What is most serious is the underdeveloped world's accusation that while it may be receiving a sop in the form of aid on the one hand, it is being bled white on the other.

Why don't all the universities in the world study the data presented by the UN Conference on Trade and Development?

If the Prebisch Report is in error, its mistakes should be exposed; if it is correct, the matter is too grave for the world to ignore.

Can anyone deny that without justice there can be no peace? Can anyone deny that to wage war in our time is to play Russian roulette with human survival?

It must amuse a North American or a European to hear that Europe and North America are in need of social revolution. All seems so secure and prosperous in their respective domains that they cannot help laughing at the overdeveloped imaginations of the underdeveloped countries, which project their own wretched problems onto the developed world.

But let us take the case of the United States, where the social revolution is already breaking out on three fronts, springing from different sources and leading to very different results: the struggle for the racial integration of the blacks; the struggle for social advancement for the thirty million Americans who live in misery in the richest country in the world; and the war against war.

The struggle for racial integration strikes me as the most inspiring chapter in the contemporary history of the United States. But though it found Christian leaders like the admirable Reverend Martin Luther King; though it has made some progress and gained appreciable adherence, sometimes on the part of the government itself, it has been in the main a long hard struggle which still demands many sacrifices and much heroism from our black brothers. How blind human beings are when their passions are involved! The United States knows how much it loses in moral stature at this most vulnerable juncture. How is it possible to speak of democracy and appear before the world as the champion of freedom while the blacks, though now equal to whites before the law, are still in practice often segregated?

The war on poverty was proclaimed by President Lyndon Johnson himself. The world admired the courage with which the Chief of State unflinchingly confessed that within the borders of that country thirty million people were living in conditions unfit for human beings.

The underdeveloped world was filled with hope. Perhaps, once the problem of integrating those thirty million into American society had been confronted and solved, the United States would throw itself heart and soul into the struggle against poverty in the rest of the world, the struggle for a civilization of harmony and unity.

I may be wrong, but the victories achieved in the United States in its war against poverty do not yet seem to be conclusive.

The root of the problem may lie in the prejudices that have pushed the United States into the arms race and into local wars that are in danger of escalating into world war at every step.

As long as Communism is seen to be the supreme evil; as long as the average American does not understand that it is an illusion to think that dying in Korea or Vietnam is the same thing as dying for the free world (an illusion because the two-thirds of humanity that live in subhuman poverty do not belong to the free world, but are enslaved by hunger, disease, ignorance, and internal colonialism); as long as the average American does not understand that several different kinds of capitalism and several different kinds of Socialism are evolving today, so that the United States and the Soviet Union are much more alike than naïve anti-Communists may think; as long as the average American does not perceive that the gravest social problem of our time is the widening gulf between the people who are becoming richer and the people who are becoming poorer; as long as there is no change in attitudes and no revolution of ideas, the United States will not be equal to the grave responsibility of being the most powerful democracy of the present day.

Hence the war against war that is surging among young Americans—in fact, among young people all over the world. How long will humanity be so barbarous as to hold as a criterion of rightness the ability to destroy?

How long will the United States use the excuse of defending human rights to allow thousands of bombers to drop tons and tons of bombs onto open cities, hitting women, children, and the sick, among others? How long will anyone in that great country admit the possibility of a repetition of Hiroshima and Nagasaki?

If you were to ask me whether I believe that education has the power to change the economic and social structures of the underdeveloped world and to make the developed world understand that it, too, is in need of social revolution, what can my answer be?

I respect those who despair of education and turn to violence. But I do not believe in hate. The problem is not one of replacing a few leaders and bringing about by force the changes that have been peacefully postponed, or peacefully written on paper, or peacefully misunderstood. Change brought about with no education to prepare the ground, no shaping of minds to receive it, is rootless. If it is not understood by those who are coerced, it breeds bitter resentment. If it is not understood by those who benefit from it, it will come to nothing because the inner preparation to use what is received was lacking.

I have a dream that will be difficult to make reality, but one that I think might lead to radical, rapid change, to creative revolution.

If the universities were to go more deeply into subjects like those raised here, and, on the hypothesis of their being valid, bring into action all the moral force at their command, that would be a most significant first step toward the educational action I have in mind.

What's more, the universities might be able to determine whether the relations between the developed and the less developed worlds are indeed out of balance, and whether the problem is in fact not one of aid but of attaining justice on a global scale by drastically revising international trade policies.

If the spiritual leaders of all religions—Christian and non-Christian alike—can meet and welcome even the collaboration of sincere and truth-loving agnostics and atheists, we can give enormous moral support to a re-evaluation of the relationship between the developed and the underdeveloped. If what is involved is indeed a question of world-wide justice, then the peace of the world is at stake.

We Christians have not begun to draw upon the richness of the truths we teach. Who is truly convinced that we are all brothers by right of having the same Heavenly Father? Who truly knows that God wanted man for His co-creator, destined to master nature and complete the task of Creation; who believes in his heart that the Church, established to carry on the work of Christ, has the duty to become incarnate like the Word of God made flesh and come to dwell among us? Who has faith that the Church has powerful forces to release in the cause of world unity and the earthly redemption of man, sign and herald of eternal redemption?

If to the activities of our universities and our spiritual leaders we add those of the written and spoken media, the cooperation of business and labor leaders, the participation of politicians and military leaders, I think we will be putting education to a decisive test as a force for democracy.

Pessimists will say that these various forces are not free: that the universities are linked to the state or to foundations, each with its own rather rigid patterns, and so have little room for maneuver; that the spiritual leaders, who receive aid from rich and influential friends, are subject to imponderable pressures more powerful than we think; that the magazines, newspapers, and radio and television stations of today are business enterprises and have only a moderate degree of independence, which leaves off where business interests begin; that the businessmen, even when, as men, they are humane and Christian, are nevertheless part of the machinery; that workers in underdeveloped areas are not free to act, for their jobs are degrading and without effective guarantees, and that those in developed areas tend to lose their revolutionary zeal as they settle into a more affluent mode of life; that political leaders are tied to their parties and military men to their codes and disciplines. . . .

It was said of Abraham that he hoped against hope. I hope not only for the help of God, Who surely will not abandon His masterpiece of creative evolution to its fate; I find a source of hope, too, in man's intelligence and common sense.

When, as will soon happen, a fact now known only to those who have studied the subject becomes apparent to all, namely, that man has the power to provide an adequate standard of living for all and, equally, that he has the power to wipe humanity off the face of the earth, it will not be possible for selfishness to have the last word.

The human instinct of self-preservation will come into play. God grant that Christians then may serve as models in overcoming selfishness and show a warmheartedness and brotherly understanding that go beyond divisions of creed, race, or ideology. God grant that we Christians may rise to the responsibility and the honor of bearing the name of Christ.

Political parties are fond of the kind of slogan that says something like: "Ride the wave of the future; come along with us." And indeed it is very important to keep up with history. Alas for anyone who attempts to breast the wave, or to swim against it.

Let us take a rapid look at one of the most important currents in the history of our time:

• After World War II there was a general feeling that the days of colonialism were numbered. It would have been futile to try to keep colonialism from being overthrown; at the most, its demise might have been ingloriously postponed. The United Nations had solemnly affirmed the rights of man; all the more reason, then, for whole peoples to arise and claim the right to control their own destiny.

• Then came the conference at Bandung. The developed world watched Asia and Africa confer together—those former colonies, those people called "backward" and "underdeveloped." It was the Third World, and at first it made many people smile, for weren't those weak continents, those subcontinents, made up of a swarm of inferior races with neither military power nor economic leverage? The more astute observers, however, followed closely what was happening in that Indonesian city and recorded the date: April 18-25, 1955.

• From year to year decisions made in the UN were more and more affected by the former colonies, without whose support it is not easy to put an idea or project into motion within that powerful organization. Significantly, one President of the UN General Assembly was a son of Ghana, a country that had not existed politically when the United Nations was born. And two years later, in 1966, the same honor fell to Tunisia.

• In the spring of 1964, the UN Conference on Trade and Development was held in Geneva—another step forward for the Third World. In spite of some hesitation and serious disagreements, it can be said that Latin America joined with Asia and Africa and, therefore, that Bandung had widened its scope. Here were seventy-five countries determined to demand that aid to the developing world be thought of in terms of world justice. It was moral strength confronting the economic and military power that had heretofore been the decisive force in human relations. It was the proclamation of the thesis of harmonious development, of civilized unity—a profoundly human, a Christian thesis.

The UN knows that the developing countries will have watched their imports rise from $22.5 billion in 1960 to $42 billion in 1970, and that during that same period the deficits of the underdeveloped countries will have risen from $1.5 billion to $15 billion. There is no doubt at all that the existing gap between the developing world and the developed countries of the East, Western Europe, and the United States is fated to grow by leaps and bounds unless international economic policies are totally transformed.

The Trade and Development Conference proved what was already known: that no country—none—gives more than one percent of its gross national product when it comes to helping the developing countries.

And please do not call this statement anti-American. The Soviet Union, which went to Geneva expecting to give orders to the Third World, had to listen to the same complaints as those made to the capitalist countries and took an equally selfish stance, declaring that it could not assume any commitment toward the developing countries on the pretext that aid, by definition, must be freely given.

The Soviet statement brings us to the gravest and most crucial point of all, one beginning in personal conviction and cresting into an irresistible wave of public opinion:

• It is not aid that we need; and in any case, aid on the order of one percent of any country's GNP is an insignificant crumb.

• If the affluent countries, East and West, Europe and the United States, are willing to pay fair prices to the developing countries for their natural resources, they can keep their aid and their relief plans.

Someone is sure to remind us at this point that the Western world does come to the aid of the developing countries.

Without the least intention of seeming ungrateful, or of trying to discover less than noble intentions behind the aid that is sent, let us clarify the issue:

• The real problem is not the fact that so far the most generous aid of any country to the Third World has not risen above one percent of its GNP.

• The real problem is not even the practical impossibility of increasing this aid to any significant degree, largely, principally even, because of the arms race.

• The really grave problem—and in this statement there is not the slightest intention of offending any government, any people, or any enterprise, but only a desire to invite an examination of conscience—the really grave problem is that the donors must ask themselves whether the money they offer is not soaked in the sweat and blood of the underdeveloped world.

An analysis in depth will alert us to the danger of throwing sand in our own eyes and trying to throw it in the eyes of others, whenever we come up against some uncomfortable truth. Is this not the case, for example, when developed countries spend fortunes on demographic research and on campaigns full of noise and fanfare to prove that development is synonymous with birth control?

It would be naïveté of the worst sort to try to ignore the acute problem of the population explosion, which is felt most tragically in the Third World. It is dishonest to reduce the rate of infant mortality, only to doom the infants whose lives are saved to a subhuman existence. But those who try to reduce development to a question of birth control are in need of psychoanalysis.

The basic statistics on world hunger are known to us all. We all know, for example, that from 1959 to 1964 the world population increased by 11.5 percent, while food production increased by only 6.5 percent. We all know that of the fifty million people who die each year, the deaths of approximately thirty-five million are caused directly by hunger or indirectly by diseases which batten on organisms already weakened by poor or insufficient food.

Even children are beginning to learn that the starvation belt girdling two-thirds of the earth takes in all of Latin America (except Argentina), Africa, the Near East (except Israel), Asia (except Japan), and Oceania (except Australia and New Zealand).

That this picture is a disgrace to Christian civilization there can be no doubt. That there is a close connection between hunger and stunted development is self-evident. But the moral problem requiring immediate analysis is whether the apparent overproduction in some countries results in genuine underconsumption in others; a consequence—can we deny it?—of superegoism.

None of this, however, gives us the right to identify nutrition, pure and simple, with development, as if it were sufficient to distribute the overabundant agricultural production of some countries to others that are starving.

It would be preferable to speak of "conquering hunger through development," without forgetting that starving peoples hunger not only for food, but also for dignity, responsibility, and freedom, and bearing in mind that "agriculture in ill-equipped countries is the driving force of progress, because there is no other source of income."

What should be our opinion of the special type of aid to the Third World which consists of sending technicians and volunteers to try to help break down the most flagrant discrepancies between the developed and the underdeveloped worlds?

I might simply point out that the experiment of transplanting capital, equipment, and battalions of highly paid technicians has been tried; but if people are not prepared for development, and if many populations are still made up of inchoate masses instead of real groups of people, then even where development blooms, it will soon wither on the vine.

No real development is possible without the humility to take the local culture into account, however rudimentary that culture may be, and without paying attention to community development, with its concomitant encouragement of the creative participation so rightly termed the keystone of development.

But if I were to say nothing more about the presence of foreign volunteers and technicians, I would be telling only one part of the truth. The other part, the great and hopeful part, which leads us to welcome young people, especially, from wealthy countries, is that this is the best possible way of deeply engaging the sympathies of the developed world in the problems of the Third World.

When one has a son or a daughter, one's own flesh and blood, in Ghana or Bolivia, in Brazil or Senegal, then this matter of development begins to take on new dimensions. And when that son or daughter returns home, we can be sure that the Third World will continue to find understanding and sympathy, love and support, in the returned volunteer.

We have reached a point at which the problem of misunderstanding stems not only from the developed countries, but to an even greater degree from internal strata of the developing countries themselves.

Unfortunately for us, the developed countries have no monopoly on egoism. With few exceptions, we in the underdeveloped countries might as well be living in the Middle Ages. Along with a few honorable exceptions, gentlemen with the mental outlook of medieval barons flourish among us. The colonial era is over, officially and politically at least. But in most developing countries internal colonialism still allows a few to enrich themselves with little effort at the expense of the masses, who eke out a subhuman existence.

Within this feudal structure, whoever comes to *help*, whether foreigner or national, will be welcomed as long as he leaves the existing unjust and inhuman system intact—welcomed all the more warmly since the dominant class is sure to benefit most from his presence.

But if someone comes along with the intention of awakening the consciousness of masses absurdly kept at a subhuman level, if he calls for human and social advancement—and for the essential structural reform to which that leads—let him be prepared to be the target of slander and defamation, for he will certainly be denounced and opposed as a Communist subversive.

We will only be playing at development as long as we remain fixed at a point which is so complex and difficult that it is almost enough to make us lose heart: until we bring about a radical reform in world trade policies, we will only be playing games.

The postulates stated here are based on such vital preoccupations that from them I have drawn ten fraternal suggestions which I will entrust to the good will and understanding of all:

1. Any and all forms of economic and social assistance to the proletariat and to proletarian nations, however broad and generous in scope they may appear to be, must, if they are not to take on a paternalistic hue, be based on a genuine respect for the intelligence and liberty of the recipient individuals and nations.

2. Included in the calculations of the cost of any investment should be a sufficient sum to compensate the human beings whose rights may otherwise be infringed upon in the name of progress and development.

3. Concerning Communism:

a. Pains should be taken to avoid the self-righteousness inherent in the kind of unilateral anti-Communism that ignores the equally inhuman results of most capitalist investment, forgetting that misery, too, can crush human beings and pervert the Divine gift of freedom into a vain and empty word.

b. It should always be remembered that the most effective way to fight Communism is by firmly and courageously facing the number one social problem of our time: the fact that two-thirds of the human race languishes in hunger and misery, and that the situation is getting worse and the percentage growing larger.

c. The day must come when we all have the serenity and courage to admit that with Socialism as with capitalism, it is no longer accurate to use the singular; we must speak of Socialisms, not Socialism, and capitalisms, not capitalism. Perhaps then we can take a step of supreme importance to humanity: we may be able, in some forms of Socialism, to separate the economic system from its materialism, a separation that is impossible in Marxist Socialism.

4. Obviously the assistance given to the Third World by the wealthy countries should not be stopped altogether simply because, in isolated circumstances and at its present level, it expresses good intentions at most and does not go to the

heart of development. Let there be a sincere effort to prove that Pope Paul's appeal in Bombay has not fallen on deaf ears: "We entrust to you our special message to the world: may the nations desist from the armaments race and turn their resources and their energies instead to fraternal assistance to the developing countries."

5. Concerning family planning, we might think in terms of an implicit pact between the underdeveloped and the developed worlds: the countries of the Third World will do all that is humanly possible, consistent with our people's psychology and religious convictions, to limit procreation within rational bounds; for their part, the wealthy nations, whose influence is decisive within the international organizations involved, will do all that is humanly possible to try to avoid the error of identifying birth control with development and the carrying out of ill-advised and indiscriminate contraceptive campaigns which are an insult to the dignity of the family.

6. Food should be consigned to the hungry with circumspection, profiting from gross errors committed with the best intentions in the past; it should be accompanied by fair and rational improvements in agriculture, along the line of those attempted by FAO.

7. Without neglecting the prime necessity of encouraging local volunteers and technicians on the higher, middle, and community organization levels, let us welcome technicians and volunteers from the wealthy countries, young people particularly. Tomorrow, when they go back home, they will form a sharp though peaceful spearhead of that social revolution in the developed world without which we can never achieve the harmonious, equitable development of this whole earth.

8. Let young Christian entrepreneurs in Europe, in a "continental dialogue" with their fellow executives of the Third World, use every legitimate means of persuasion to get the latter to appreciate and accept the development of social consciousness among their workers, for such *conscientização* can only be authentic if it is effective, and it cannot be called

effective unless it leads to reforms in inhuman social and economic structures.

9. In moments of decision nonviolent action, the peaceful weapon of the developing countries, must receive an echo and support in the developed world. Let us take care that the emerging masses do not lose their belief in democracy but keep their trust in Love, in Justice, and in Peace.

10. If what I have proposed seems too ambitious, I am willing to forget the first nine suggestions I have made, provided the tenth and last is taken to heart. I make it now and let it speak for me, because it goes to the very heart of our subject:

• Let young Christian executives take up the all but impossible challenge of a drastic reform in international trade policies.

• If today's executives lack the understanding or the courage to do so, I pray that tomorrow's executives will be less dismayed by this colossal task.

• May they have the backbone to fight the trusts, which are more powerful today than the most powerful states; their oppressive acts, especially their actions in the developing countries, cry out to heaven. May their eyes be opened to the fact that in the Third World exploitation on the part of international trusts—which crush fledgling local industries, show no qualms at bleeding the poor nations of more than they receive, and threaten to introduce automation into our underdeveloped areas—blatant exploitation by these international trusts is arousing antipathy and loathing for the very phrase "private enterprise" and inciting indiscriminate, unjust hatred against all employers, good and bad.

The UN Conference on Trade and Development, held in Geneva from March to June of 1964, constitutes one of the best and most constructive contributions for future development. One day history will do justice to CEPAL, the Economic Council for Latin America, which was farsighted enough to see the need for this meeting and to arrange for it through the

United Nations. At long last the nub of the problem was reached. It was a dispassionate and objective indictment, backed up by statistics, of the imbalance in the relations between the developed and the underdeveloped worlds. There was no bitterness, no demagoguery. No ingratitude, no one-sided accusations. The other aspects of development were not neglected, but it was made clear beyond the shadow of a doubt that:

- It is not enough to prove that the developed countries are not contributing even one percent of their GNP to the underdeveloped world.
- It is still not enough to prove that war and the arms race devour, and will go on devouring, sums several times bigger than those allocated for development.
- The problem is not one of raising development assistance to one or two percent, for it is not a question of aid, but of justice on a global scale.

The world was shocked when Raúl Prebisch showed that in the last ten years Latin America has been bled of more than $13 billion.

History will record the equally deplorable selfishness of the Soviet Union and the United States, for neither power made the response called for by the gravity of the indictment and both tried their best to torpedo it. However, it is even more urgent to put an end to the injustice—and I repeat, *on a global scale*—than it is to destroy the stockpile of nuclear bombs.

History will record that several years after this remarkable assembly it was still not possible to create in the United Nations a real World Trade Organization to complement UNESCO and OIT. So far we have had to be satisfied with a Council for Trade and Development.

Honor is due the Ecumenical Council, Vatican II, which, after leaving ample scope for the development that Pope John XXIII described in *Pacem in Terris* as the greatest social problem of our time, observed very carefully what went on in

Geneva and threw its full support behind the thesis advanced by CEPAL. In the "Pastoral Constitution on the Presence of the Church in the World," the Council declared:

The international community must organize and stimulate development, but in such a way that the funds set aside for it are applied as efficiently and equitably as possible. Without putting the right to establish subsidiaries in jeopardy, it is also encumbent upon this community to organize world economic relationships in such a way that they may develop in accordance with the norms of justice. Adequate institutions should be created to promote and regulate international trade, above all with the less developed nations, and to compensate for defects proceeding from a gross inequality of power among nations. Such an organization, conjoined to technical, cultural, and financial aid, should furnish sufficient subsidies to those nations setting out on the road to development to enable them to achieve a balanced increment in their economies.

At first glance it may seem foolish, even absurd, to dream of making a good and just idea prevail over economic interests that are stronger than the strongest states. But history is full of examples of ideas carrying the most apparently insuperable interests before them. On a national level, we need look no further than the abolition of slavery, led by young men like the poet Castro Alves and the statesmen Rui Barbosa and Joaquim Nabuco. Internationally, we need only look at the gains made by the workers.

One campaign can no longer be postponed: that is, a second abolition of slavery to add to the political independence of our people the indispensable economic independence, not only of a few social groups and regions, but of the complete man and of all men.

This emancipation cannot be postponed, for it is no exaggeration to say that world peace is at stake. Our youth, our youth above all, have lost patience and are turning to desperate, violent, and radical causes. There is no time to be lost: we must prove to them that the democratic process is valid. We must make a mighty effort to save our countries from shameful and inhuman civil wars and to save humanity from a global conflict whose consequences none can foresee.

One day a European who manages a steel mill in my country invited me to visit the plant, giving me leave to open all the doors, all the desk drawers, all the books. Afterward he asked me what I thought of the mill. In answer, I said: "I think I've seen everything good about your factory: safety measures; salaries; provision for education, health, recreation. The only thing I don't understand is the reason for the invisible warnings all over the mill that say: 'Worker, all will be given you in exchange for the bourgeois luxuries of freedom and intelligence.' "

My friend, who is a good man and an intelligent one, smiled sadly and remarked: "You're right. But what can I do? When the two of us are talking, each of us is a human being. When I meet with the Brazilian Board of Directors, I am only a fraction: one-eighteenth, to be exact. When I go to Europe and take part in a company meeting, I'm nothing but one cog in the machinery."

The problem faced by any private enterprise in dealing with its workers becomes even more acute when it is operating in one of the proletarian nations of the Third World: there is no difficulty in bestowing benefits on the workers, as long as they use their intelligence and freedom sparingly. . . .

The impasse between the two worlds of development and underdevelopment, and the virtual inability of the developed world to understand the angle from which we view the relationship between our two worlds, raises a question that touches on what is perhaps the gravest economic problem of national scope.

However much it may be in our interest to learn from the experience of the economically developed nations, Brazil will have to find its own way out of its underdevelopment. Pope John warned:

Political communities in the throes of economic development naturally possess their own unmistakable individuality, by reason not only of their resources and the specific nature of their environment, but also deriving from their traditions, rich in human values, and the characteristic qualities of the members of their societies. When the economically developed countries come to their aid, they should be perceptive enough to discern and respect this individuality and to conquer the temptation to project their own image onto the developing countries.

Oddly enough, every so often in the developed world we find someone who understands us. Take, for instance, a passage from *The Rich Nations and the Poor Nations* by Barbara Ward, a respected economist and one of the finest human beings of our age. Here is what she says:

Wealth coupled to indifference draws down upon itself the classic punishment: that is, through indifference and hardness of heart, to lose contact with the longings of the great masses of humanity. This loss of sensibility can happen to anyone, as history makes plain. Today, however, we are witnessing a new phenomenon: the rich communities are becoming the victims of this same deficiency in human understanding.

Observing that the English and Americans do a good deal of talking about freedom and are determined to fight to defend the free world, Barbara Ward brings an indictment against forms of slavery that often go unperceived, such as the enslavement to misery, ignorance, and disease.

She wonders anxiously what forces will be strong enough to induce the wealthy countries to shake off their comfortable lethargy long enough to re-examine the totally new footing on which it will be necessary to establish relations among human beings. They cannot look for very much help from the common run of their economists.

What experience of underdevelopment can writers have who are born and brought up in abundance? When they hear talk of masses eking out a miserable, subhuman existence, how can we expect them to reason except in terms of racial inferiority, physical disability, or laziness, assumptions which will prompt them to set up aid programs, at best? Demands for justice must sound to their ears like incredible impertinence and base ingratitude.

Now that it is starting out on its own path, Brazil must take care to avoid in its own economic planning the use of the very principles which are in great part responsible for the growing gap between the two worlds. To take their validity for granted and continue to make use of them will only initiate or aggravate, in this country, the same forms of discrimination which we deplore when they are committed on a world-wide scale.

Here are two examples among many:

- The principle that the best investment is the one, wherever and whenever made, which will yield maximum profits, with minimum effort and maximum speed.
- The principle that economics is a value in itself, capable, in its own good time, of bringing all good things.

7

Latin America: Christian Half
of the Underdeveloped World

It is easy to take for granted that Latin America is and always will be the Catholic continent, the world's reservoir of Christianity. But the Latin-American masses—with us, without us, or against us—are beginning to open their eyes. Today isolated peoples no longer exist; there are no more walls. The communications media mock any attempt at isolation; and woe to Christianity on the day the eyes of the masses are opened, if they believe themselves to have been abandoned to the great and powerful with the connivance of the Church.

The question is not one of prestige. Our obligation is to serve; it is our human, Christian duty to help lead the children of God out of the subhuman state in which they live. Misery degrades human life and is an outrage to the Creator and Father.

And here is where prudence enters the scene: it is far quicker and easier to open the eyes of the masses, to awaken their consciousness to the conditions around them, than to bring about structural reform. So the onlookers say, wringing their hands, that anyone who, knowing this, stirs the masses to social awareness is playing into the hands of subversives, and, since he is pitting one class against another, is doing the Communists' work for them.

It is amazing to what lengths people will go in defense of

their privileges. It would indeed be doing the Marxists' work for them to maintain religion as the opiate of the people and as an "alienated and alienating" Church. But how can we ignore what is strong and fine, what is meaningfully democratic and full of the sap of Christianity, in the effort to awaken consciousness?

It is a question of raising human beings to their feet; of arousing their initiative, cooperative efforts, leadership; accustoming them not to expect everything to come from the central government. Misery, when handed down from father to son and grandfather to grandson, leaves marks that are difficult to erase.

The man who depends on others for everything, who is a pariah, an object of protective social welfare but not a subject exercising his just rights, who is at the mercy of the good will, or ill will, of an all-powerful master for whom there is no law, authority, or justice, since everything and everyone depends on his whims, is no more than a slave. How can he help sinking into fatalism? What hope has he of escaping from discouragement, despair, and wretchedness today and rebellion tomorrow? Certainly not merely by learning to read and write, even if the sham of a right to vote is thrown in for good measure.

When the Church proclaims, as it did in Mar del Plata, that the socioeconomic structures of this continent are unjust and in urgent need of rapid and radical reform, it is not with the intention of evading our share of responsibility for the deplorable situation Latin America is in today: as the supreme spiritual force of the Christian continent, we could and should have done our part to bring about a far more just and humane state of things.

Once we children of God in Latin America have made up our minds to participate in the development and integration of this continent, we can carry out programs which would call forth an echo of response throughout its whole extent. For instance:

- We must make our countries independent economically in order to complete the political independence that was the triumph of our national heroes. In the case of Brazil, we must complete the work begun on September 7, 1822, the date on which our independence was proclaimed.

- We must abolish slavery once and for all. Once the Americas were free of the shame of African slavery, we began enslaving our own fellow countrymen. Brazil must complete the emancipation proclaimed on May 13, 1888.

Once they have determined to play an active role in the development and integration of this country, Brazil's children of God have immediate and specific campaigns to carry out, such as:

- To petition the government for the funds the Workers' Court of Justice must have if it is to live up to its fine name and begin to take a decisive role in the just and human development of our less developed areas, particularly the Northeast.

- To petition the public authorities to demonstrate real understanding, so that the workers can have genuine unions capable of making a valid contribution in establishing justice.

When we Latin Americans compare our problems with those of the African and Asian countries now emerging from colonialism, we are surprised to discover how similar are the difficulties that lie ahead: we are mature enough to perceive the gulf lying between political independence and its economic counterpart, mature enough to understand the diverse and often subtle forms neo-colonialism can take.

Though the immediate struggle for existence will probably continue to lead to competition and clashes among the nations of these continents for some time, the day will come when we shall discover cogent reasons for making the Third World a reality.

If this is true, it is no less true that Latin America is spiritually linked to the wealthy countries. This truth may make us shudder, but the prosperous part of the world—that is, the 20 percent of humanity that reaps the fruits of the labor of the other 80 percent—is either Christian or of Christian origin.

Since Providence permits our continent to belong simultaneously to the Third World and to the wealthy nations—to the Third World by reason of our material difficulties and to the prosperous countries by reason of our Christian origin—can it be that God has reserved to us a special mission to mediate between these two quarreling worlds?

While by no means forgetting the admirable young Christian communities of Africa and Asia, it is we Latin Americans who bear the responsibility of constituting the Christian majority of the Third World.

It is a source of grief to realize that our brothers in Africa and Asia almost invariably believe Christianity to be the religion of the white men: the religion of the oppressors who only yesterday dominated their lives and almost invariably exploited them; who even today have not been able to make up their minds to help the rest of the world with more than a few pitiful crumbs, never more than one percent of their gross national product; who, out of ambition, vanity, disbelief in the power of love, or delusions of defending freedom and human dignity, persist in an arms race which cancels out the effect of any development-aid programs they contribute; and who, through the wretched prices they impose on raw materials, still extort far more than they help.

Christians in Latin America have an awful responsibility:

• Toward our affluent brethren in Christ, we must have enough love to try to help them free themselves from their selfishness, their excessive fixation on ease and the ephemeral, their pragmatic materialism, and make them aware of the danger of being a scandal in the eyes of our non-Christian brothers and conveying to them the most erroneous ideas about Christ and His doctrine.

• As for ourselves, while keeping our eyes open to the perilous fascination of Marxism, which exerts so strong an attraction on workers and university students, it is our duty to fight for development and to try to learn from the lessons that the development ethic is desperately trying to teach the wealthy countries. It is our duty to try to bring about a new dimension in development—a Christian dimension, strong enough to pull us out of our miserable subhuman state without letting us fall into the inhumanity of excessive comfort and luxury. We must learn to teach the lesson that a plenitude of good is the very opposite of a proliferation of goods.

The gravest economic problem of our time is this urgent need to look at the relations between the developed and the underdeveloped countries from a new angle. As long as the developed world thinks in terms of aid, as long as it is not persuaded that what is at stake is universal justice, there will be no understanding among the peoples of the world, no peace on earth; for peace without justice is a delusion.

Latin America is the Christian half of the underdeveloped world. Latin America should serve as an example of that respect for the basic rights of human beings so deplorably disregarded by internal colonialism. And Brazil has special obligations in Latin America, as the Northeast does in Brazil. I have said before and I repeat now that those with legal training have a very special role to play in the campaign for a more highly developed and humane society.

In the developing Northeast, it is not enough for them to mouth the legalistic formulas of developed countries. They must use their creative imagination and their spirit of invention to create new laws, or make new applications of perennial laws, to meet new situations.

Because we are a part of Brazil and of Latin America, we must shoulder our responsibility as the Christian portion, the Christian continent, of the Third World. Obviously, it would be absurd to consider that this makes us greater or better than our brothers of Asia and Africa. But we do have a greater responsibility. Christianity must inspire us with the desire to serve, so that as we develop we do not become more selfish and overbearing.

This warning is not an empty one. Let us have the courage to remind ourselves that while we see slogans against foreign imperialism on the walls of our cities, the capitals of Paraguay and Bolivia are placarded with slogans against Brazilian imperialism.

Real brotherhood on this continent, fraternal friendship with the rest of the Third World, and brotherly dialogue with the developed world is the witness for Christ by Latin America that will be most easily understood by our African and Asian brothers.

The Third World will be making a fatal mistake if it does no more than point out the defects in the attitude of the wealthy countries while remaining blind to its own faults, which are no less serious and fundamental.

Two of the most pernicious and most justly singled out are these:

- The present structure of our societies, which ensures that the aid that is received benefits a plutocracy long proved incapable, for the most part, of yielding any of its own privileges for the common welfare.
- Dishonesty, which not infrequently diverts to private interests what should serve the common good.

It is incredibly difficult to get reforms under way, particularly when a society wishes to work within a democratic framework. The first battle, that of finding suitable textbook methods to follow, is surpassed in difficulty by the second, that of putting into practice reforms approved in theory.

In practice, what will happen to the land statute? How much will the government be able to do as regards income-tax and fiscal reform? When and how will the government put into practice the national housing plan for which it has such high hopes?

Brazil: Development and Underdevelopment

Brazil, synthesis of the world, grows and develops in spite of everything and everyone. Today it offers the possibility, for those with greatness of soul, of living a thousand lives in one lifetime. For within its borders Brazil has both developed and developing areas, as well as those that are openly and scandalously undeveloped, and even areas that are not occupied at all. Brazil can and should teach the world to take part in the most significant dialogue of this century: the dialogue between development and underdevelopment.

Everyone in our country understands and proclaims the urgency of basic reforms, but many people were suspicious of those who attempted to carry them out and fearful of Communist infiltration. Now that the situation has changed, we have no time to lose. May the longed-for reforms come without delay. May they be just and fair, but, above all, may they in no way substitute lip service for substance.

May the reforms come without the necessity for coercion and, above all, without confrontations and bitterness. May the Brazilian people remain forever incapable of hate, that greatest sin of all, want of love; for God is charity, God is love!

We have now reached the midpoint in the decade of development for the Northeast. In spite of everything and everyone (and none of us is completely guiltless of sins against our region's development), the Northeast will grow. Instead of taking the reactionary position of those who see an insuperable dichotomy between agriculture and industrialization, you will be activists for agricultural industrialization and help others see development as a synthesis.

What is the true significance of calling Brazil an essentially agricultural nation? The statement should in no way imply maintaining the inglorious position of keeping our rural masses in a subhuman state. One of the characteristics of a developing country is that it obtains, from a smaller and smaller number of real farmers, incomparably more than could be produced by rural peasants, who are more like the cactus than like true children of God.

Who, for example, does not sense, does not know, that without the Paulo Afonso hydroelectric plant SUDENE would not exist, since one of the basic parts of the infrastructure essential to the progress of our region would be lacking? On this fact rests the interest with which we follow the fulfillment of the long-range plan to bring electricity to the Northeast, one of the most authentic proofs of our capacity for pulling ourselves up by our own bootstraps. We follow with interest the activities of the São Francisco Hydroelectric Company, the Rural Electric Company of the Northeast, the Boa Esperança Hydroelectric Company, the National Drought Control Bureau, and those twenty-one business firms and sixty-four combines under the general control of SUDENE which, if properly funded, will make it possible for us to look from a new perspective at agriculture in the new Northeast.

On that day when developed Brazil has been persuaded that the most intelligent course it can take is to lead undeveloped Brazil into development—for then and only then will it have the internal market that is vital to its productivity—we Brazilians will have attained the experience and the moral strength to intervene in the dialogue between the developed and the developing worlds.

Why should it not fall to us as a people to set an example by proclaiming the right to development, with the concomitant duty of eradicating underdevelopment, and this less in terms of aid and favors than in terms of justice?

Why should it not fall to us as a people to set an example by living out our development as our entire population, and every subgroup of which it is composed, passes from a less to a more human stage of life?

Of course we will not be content with vague words. "Less human stage" applies to all the privations humanity is heir to, from material want to moral and spiritual deprivation. The expression "less human stage" extends to all types of oppressive structures: the misuse of power and the misuse of possessions; administrative corruption; exploitation both of and by the workers; chicanery; speculation. . . .

"More human stage" is synonymous with obtaining the essentials for life: food, health, shelter, clothing, education, fair working conditions, and spiritual guidance. "More human stage" also means, and that most particularly, belief in our Heavenly Father, faith in Christ, and the practice of charity.

Why should it not fall to us as a people to set an example by confronting the problems of economic development with firmness and decision, and adding to it social development and the opening of wider perspectives for the deifying expansion that only Divine Grace has the power to bring about?

Now is the time to mobilize this country to do all in its power to ensure that no part of our territory, no part of our population, feels segregated, left out of the life of our nation.

There are in our country derelict areas which are struggling heroically to take a real part in national life: the underdeveloped areas of the Northeast, the Central Plateau, Amazônia. Whole groups of people are stranded far from the mainstream. Think of the millions of Brazilians in our rural areas who live in subhuman conditions, not to mention those who flee to the great cities and remain imprisoned there in the huts of the *favelas* (slums).

They are outside the mainstream because they lack the minimum prerequisites for active participation in the life of their country. They are not even in a condition to participate passively, in the sense of receiving those benefits that our laws and institutions promise every Brazilian, such as an elementary education. These marginal groups take no part in collective decisions, nor do they receive goods and services from the community.

Let us not forget that the sum total of all the segregated, crushed human beings does not add up to authentic integration. It is just as true that man is the subject, beginning, and end of society as that a country's integration is false and illusory unless it begins with the inner integration of each of its sons.

We want a Brazil that is one whole entity, with no part of it abandoned to its fate, a child neglected in his own house. If we dream of a union of the whole human family, let us begin with national union, with no one in the shadows, no one forgotten, no one abandoned.

Though no expert in economics, we reject as anti-human the theory of investing always and exclusively where profits are highest, quickest, and safest. It is this selfish theory that continues to widen the shocking, explosive gap between the developed and the underdeveloped.

It is well that the South is beginning to understand more clearly that helping to develop the Northeast is not merely a fraternal gesture but a proof of intelligence and a matter of self-interest: when the thirty million people of the Northeast acquire purchasing power, they will constitute the ideal internal market for the industrial South.

And what is true for the Northeast is just as true for the North and the Central Plateau.

No one can any longer hold back the development of our underdeveloped areas. We have the bureaus of regional planning, headed by SUDENE, the Superintendency for the Development of the Northeast; the Central Brazil Foundation; the Southwest Frontier; the Superintendency for Amazonian Development. And most important, we have, especially in our own Northeast, the determination of our people. Development is as necessary to them as the air they breathe.

Within its borders Brazil epitomizes the world: the developed South cannot cope with the developing Northeast, North, and

Central Plateau. The day we can sensitize the minds and hearts of Southern businessmen, the day they really understand how essential it is to help developing Brazil as brothers, on that day we will be in a moral position to talk as equals to the developed world.

At first glance it all looks so clear, so simple: if the Northeast needs the South to cooperate in its development, so does the South need a developed Northeast, without which it will lack the internal market that is vital to its burgeoning industries. If there were any logic to human relations, this convergence of interests would rapidly lead to a meshing of gears.

But in practice, it appears to be easier to make imperialist gestures toward Paraguay and Bolivia than to facilitate the genuine advancement of the Northeast that would presage the advancement of Amazônia.

True, the government has created incentives for investment in the developing areas. What, then, is lacking? Is there no intelligent, skillful promotion of the offered facilities? Is SU-DENE, as the guiding organization for interested investors, not as dynamic as it might be? Or is the explanation to be found in the fact that SUDENE has suffered losses of key personnel and therefore no longer finds it possible to examine carefully enough the projects submitted to it?

Perhaps we could set in motion a public opinion campaign in three stages:

1. We men of the Northeast could meet to study the next guidelines put out by SUDENE. We would examine critically its method of setting priorities and the machinery for carrying out projects. From political parties we would demand that Northeastern development programs—especially SUDENE—be seen as above party and regional interests, and solely in terms of the common good.

2. Developed Brazil and developing Brazil could hold a fraternal meeting, preferably in a developing area. Recife's doors and heart would be open for it. And who knows? This might offer a splendid opportunity for a visit from Paul VI.

Of all men on earth, the Pope is one of the most sensitive to the struggle for development, as is proved by his recent pilgrimage to India.

3. We Brazilians could start a public-opinion campaign in the developing world: newspapers exchanging views with one another, television stations with other television stations, universities with universities. To doubt that a well-thought-out program along these lines would be successful is to cast doubt on the essential validity of democratic methods.

Once when I was in the United States I took advantage of the climate of genuine freedom which is not only permitted but cherished there; and when I was heatedly denouncing the subtle forms of neo-colonialism practiced by North Americans in Latin America, an interruption called my attention to the internal colonialism which is devouring us Latin Americans from within.

Applying this comment to Brazil, I tried to assume that it was an allusion to the industry of the South. We know that our own South owes its expansion largely to profitable exploitation of raw materials from the North and the Northeast.

But it was made clear to me that the internal colonialism alluded to was that of rural areas where, with few exceptions, Brazilians were enriching themselves at the expense of other Brazilians whom they kept in a situation as bad as, or worse than, that of the old African or Asiatic colonies.

Ever since then, I have been tormented by the idea that the rural landlords who uphold internal colonialism, those I heard denounced in the United States, must derive conscious or unconscious support from the fact that the condition of those dwelling on diocesan lands is often no better.

And so there is an illusory and dangerous form of collusion between the two: the bishop, unable to better the situation on his own Church land, too easily accepts the continuation of this medieval system of feudal baronies under another name. And it is in the Big House that the priest usually celebrates

Mass for the descendants of the slaves in the cabins. . . .

As for the landlord, he is at peace with his soul and thinks of himself as a bulwark of order and of Christian principles.

Are we acting as real friends, I will say, not only to the farm workers and the tenant farmers, but even to the landlords? Is a friend one who fosters illusions or one who tries to make his friend face reality?

It would be cruel for us to assume the pharisaical pose of not confessing candidly at the outset that this ambiguous and untenable situation has its origin in our own province.

Here, too, we will put forward specific and, I hope, feasible suggestions. But there is still a third fault of which we stand accused.

As human beings and Christians, we cannot but thrill to the idea of progress. God made us in His own image, and He is not a petty, jealous God. Having entrusted man with finishing the work of Creation, He feels a Father's thrill of pride at seeing His Steward splitting the atom, sprinkling the sky with stars, and mastering nature.

And yet human selfishness makes of progress a cruel thing. For instance, automation in developed countries makes more people jobless every month, though industry—if not that of peace, then that of war—absorbs the unemployed victims of the electronic and cybernetic age.

When automation comes to a less developed country, however, the victims of progress clearly run the risk of falling by the wayside.

A specific example will make this clear. How can we help rejoicing at the redeeming prospects opening up for the agro-industry of sugar in the Northeast? We must take care, however, not to sin by omission by failing to sound a warning of what will happen to the rural workers on land left fallow as a consequence of the modernization of the sugar mills.

As a rule, the yield will be three or four times that of today, on a fourth of the acreage now being cultivated. On the other hand, the number of workers will as a rule be cut to half the present number, or even to a third or a fourth. And it is obvious that the millowner will keep, not the least able-bodied men, but the strongest and most skillful. For the first time in the history of the Northeast, rural workers will be a hand's breadth away from becoming real men, only a step away from being transformed from yesterday's pariahs into the middle class of tomorrow—provided, that is, that ownership of a piece of land freed by the mill is accompanied by the necessary services: technical, financial, social, and spiritual.

If this assistance is lacking, where can the former mill workers turn? Most of them will be over thirty-five, most of them will lack even a minimum of specialized training, and most of them will have large numbers of children. However many industries come to the Northeast, these subworkers' turn will never come and they will be doomed to fall by the wayside.

In view of this description of a situation in Brazil which is probably the same, or very similar, in other countries on this continent, let us make a pact among ourselves to do all that is humanly possible to cease lending ourselves unwittingly as a cover-up for what is indefensible.

Our place as Latin-American bishops in the world hierarchy is an odd one. On the one hand, our hunger and thirst for justice cannot, thank God, be denied; nor can our open position in favor of a form of human and Christian advancement going beyond mere social-welfare work. On the other hand, we have not, we cannot, slough off the vexing, embarrassing encumbrance of our heritage of medieval privileges and immunities.

If Brazilians are not led skillfully and gently—lovingly— they can never be coerced. Fiscal pressure and confiscation are not a good road to agrarian reform.

Everything said here springs from a conviction that the battle for development is joined and that victory is in the offing. But that does not mean that there are not grave difficulties to be overcome.

We have the impression that not everyone in the Brazilian

government understands the deep, underlying reason for the creation of SUDENE: the necessity of treating unequal regions unequally, as the only expedient capable of enabling this country to achieve whole, harmonious development.

Powerful forces are lobbying to see that investments are made by preference where they will yield the highest, safest, quickest profit. If this is done, regions that are already developed will become more prosperous, and underdeveloped regions will sink further into bankruptcy.

A whole concept of life, a whole philosophy of development, are at stake. Anyone who, like Pope John XXIII, understands that the dialogue between the developed and the underdeveloped worlds is the gravest social problem of our time, must wish to lend his fraternal aid to developing Brazil; and this in the name of victory over selfishness, of peace between classes, and even of national unity.

Anyone who understands people and truly respects them knows it is useless to think of development unless the people are prepared to carry it out, or at least to take part in it.

When will every public officeholder in this country understand that a cut in the budget of a public bureau in a developed area is not nearly as grave as a cut in the budget of a bureau like SUDENE, whose *raison d'être* is to serve as a lever for progress in the Northeast? Is it so very hard to understand what development is? Is it so very hard to understand the Northeast?

I do not have the competence to evaluate the results of the present policy of controlled inflation. I can only bring to the attention of those responsible for our economic policies—whose good intentions we have no reason to doubt—the testimony of one who lives among the people, who bears witness to the fact that life is getting harder for them, and who hears their cries of protest, unscreened by the flattering filters that surround those who govern, in every place and every time.

Are our domestic business firms mistaken when they think that the credit restrictions which are choking the life out of them are not imposed on foreign firms? If their impression is true, are there in fact reasons that outweigh the stifling of incentive for the youthful industries of a youthful country?

Is it really softheaded sentimentality to be shocked by the growing number of bankruptcies? Is it demagogy to talk about the hunger which is now spreading to the middle class? Or is our economic planning following a deterministic line that won't let us call a halt? Is it simply taken for granted that the crushing of millions of human beings is inevitable on the road to wealth, that personal and collective tragedies are an inevitable, reasonable, and even advantageous price to pay for the abundance that lies just around the corner?

With my thoughts on those who are shocked at my incursions into the realm of the temporal, all of which are motivated by love of man and love of God, I take the liberty of quoting the Ecumenical Council once more:

Development should be left neither to the almost mechanical course of individual economic activity, nor solely to the power of public authority. We should combat as errors not only those theories which, in the guise of false liberty, make the necessary reforms more difficult, but also those which sacrifice the fundamental rights of individuals or groups to the collective organization of production.

Shouldn't our economic policy-makers take into consideration data such as that furnished by Raúl Prebisch to the UN or culled from official U.S. statistics?

It is obvious that the task of improving Brazil's economic prospects should not devolve wholly on our economists, even if economists from all parts of the country got together and worked as a team. It is equally true that economists from the developed and the developing worlds cannot be made solely responsible for the effort of putting the relations between the two worlds into their rightful terms. Public opinion must be aroused: the universities should join the campaign, and so should other vital groups interested in world peace, such as leaders of every religion, the written and spoken media, leading business executives, labor leaders, political leaders.

But the economists have a special place in this movement, for it is up to them to provide data, interpret facts, and discover valid arguments, since the main battles will be joined in their area of competence. They cannot gain greater authority than by freeing themselves of "economics-ism" and discovering the natural and indestructible alliance between development and humanism. Allow me to suggest a few possible lines of action. They should try to equip themselves to demonstrate to their Marxist colleagues that alienation has two faces: forgetting the economic side is no less an error than trying to reduce all the immense complexity of human life to a question of economics. It is a demonstrable fact that humanism without God becomes inhuman, anti-human. It is not a question of finding an escape hatch for our ignorance and an excuse for the self-centered positions we adopt. It is a question of accepting reality: just as strong as the economic urge that makes us want to get the most by expending the least amount of effort, just as strong as the aesthetic urge, and the scientific, and political, and social urges, is the religious urge, which imbues man with a thirst that only the Absolute can slake.

Do economists seek a good beginning for the revolution to be waged against economics for the sake of economics, which only makes the rich countries richer and the poor countries poorer? Let them fight for the recognition that the most fruitful investments are those linked directly to the formation of man. Give man his due as the focus and end of economic activity. Help Brazil take on the awesome challenge of creating full employment for all Brazilians, without letting any part of our territory remain outside our national economic life.

We are standing at the threshold of an age of increasing automation, of cybernetics, of unprecedented developments in every field, all of which are adding even more complexity and excitement to the equation which it will be mainly up to the economists to formulate.

It should be no part of our intention to imitate, in respect to sister developing areas, the selfish attitudes which have caused us so much suffering. We can and should have respect for Amazônia. It is easy to repeat glibly that Amazônia is a living chapter of Genesis. But our Creator and Father made man His partner in Creation. Didn't we conquer the Paulo Afonso Falls and transform them into the admirable source of energy they always were in the mind of God? Didn't we build the Furnas and Três Marias Dams, and aren't we building others like Boa Esperança and Celusa—the former bringing new life, new hope, new prospects for the future to Piauí and Maranhão; the second, that gigantic Urubupungá Hydroelectric System destined to be one of the greatest electric-power-generating plants in the world, setting off an accelerated process of development over an area which includes a considerable part of the states of São Paulo, Mato Grosso, and Minas Geraes, with inevitable repercussions in the whole region—the entire country, in fact? Didn't we achieve the colossal feat of laying the Belém-Brasília Highway, dropping the first workmen by parachute in order to open this redeeming road through virgin forest? These are the kinds of battles that Brazil understands. This is the only kind of war that suits the character of our people and the Christian spirit implanted within us: the war against misery, the battle of development.

Let me repeat: we must make up our minds to incorporate every part of our territory and every group in our population into effective, normal participation in our national life. Wherever there are subhumans, subworkers, sublife, it must be our task to help these masses become people and then, with no transition, see that these people have a real part in our development.

Is it possible to speak with a straight face about development in the Amazon region?

A technician from that part of the country once gave me a valuable lesson. He said: "It's thrilling to see the Northeast throwing itself heart and soul into the fight for development. But it's disheartening for us in the North to hear the *nordestinos* say: 'Oh, Amazônia's still a chapter from Genesis.' "

And the young technician begged the *nordestinos* on no account to adopt the selfish position of struggling to improve the Northeast while leaving Amazônia to its fate, on no account to give currency to the myth of a slumbering Amazônia. And then came the challenging invitation: "Let the Northeast join forces with the North to fight like brothers, side by side, to free ourselves from underdevelopment!"

The Northeast should accept Amazônia's fraternal invitation: they should join forces to hammer out a common destiny.

There are sure to be those who smile ironically at this pact, which may look like an alliance between a man in rags and a man in tatters. But it is a step forward when the weak no longer mock the weak; when, instead of draining strength from one another, each gives of himself and the two unite to become one.

But won't Amazônia, simply because it is such a colossus, be too great a burden for our frail shoulders?

There are sure to be pessimists who think that the only honest thing to do is to admit our own incapacity and hand over this world to the supermen, the masters of advanced technology who in a few years can bring about an awakening which would take us centuries to accomplish.

But no: Brazil is proving itself quite able to assume responsibility for its own destiny, to master and tame the riches entrusted to it by God.

Before there was any Paulo Afonso power plant, the celebrated phrase of the novelist José Lins do Rêgo was famous: "The Paulo Afonso Falls have shouted themselves hoarse awaiting the coming of Brazilian engineers."

Well, the Brazilian engineers finally got there. And they built not only Paulo Afonso, but Três Marias and Furnas, and they are building Boa Esperança and Celusa, to mention only the key dams. Then came the epic feat of planting Brasília in the heart of the Central Plateau in a space of four years.

And the colossal feat of slashing the Belém-Brasília Highway through the heart of the jungle. That road, which the pessimists said would be abandoned to the jaguars in three years, will never again be closed.

Who taught the Brazilian engineers such intelligence, such pioneer spirit, such daring? Did they work with purebred Aryan supermen, abounding in health and exuding supernutrition? They must indeed have worked with a super-race; for to have accomplished what was accomplished, with undernourished men in poor health, is proof positive that these Brazilian mestizos, these half-breed *caboclos,* these dumb *nordestinos,* are not an inferior race. They may not have a giant's physique, but they certainly have a giant's fortitude. We need not be afraid to say that Amazônia is ours, and in our hands it will never be a vast, unproductive landed estate.

But all this gives rise to an insidious question which we make a point of facing head on: does religion have any strengths to bring to this struggle, or does it hinder more than it helps?

Nature overwhelms man. How can we feel like anything but pygmies in the middle of the Amazon's river-sea, where all attempts to measure distances around us are futile? Is it not alienating to think of God in such a place? Is it not better to help the man of Amazônia to forget the next life and cling to this one instead; to help him forget God so that he can make the most of himself?

When malaria strikes, isn't making a promise to a saint in return for recovery a cowardly form of escapism on the part of a man who doesn't know how to use his head? When terrible injustices make absolute masters, semigods, of a few, and wretched pariahs of the many, isn't religion a hindrance because it teaches patience instead of revolt, preaches love when it ought to preach hate, and demands respect for an order that is nothing more nor less than stratified injustice?

The only people who are impressed by such statements are those who confuse religion with superstition and do not have the happiness of understanding the true meaning of the Christian Message. There is no question that we Christians are frail and lukewarm and all too often sorry witnesses of our faith. But there is also no question but that Christ is the Friend who will never fail us, and that from genuine Christianity springs a strong and beautiful urge toward development.

The Master liked to teach through parables which made a deep impression on the minds of His hearers and which seem equally pertinent today. Will you allow me to present some of the essential points in the mystique of development through incidents, anecdotes, and parables?

When Getúlio Vargas wanted to encourage the state of Maranhão by the example of Piauí, he went to São Luiz (the capital of Maranhão) and told the story of two teamsters.

Both men were driving heavy loads. The roads were muddy, and both carts got stuck. One of the teamsters was a devout man. He fell on his knees in the mud and begged God to help him. He prayed and prayed without ceasing, his eyes turned heavenward.

Meanwhile the other man blasphemed like fury, but he was working all the time. He picked up sticks of wood, leaves, and handfuls of dirt. He hit his donkey. He tried to push the cart. He cursed.

Just then a miracle happened: an angel floated down from on high. But to the surprise of both men, he came to the aid of the blasphemous teamster. The poor man was embarrassed and exclaimed: "Pardon me, but you must be mistaken. The help must be meant for that fellow over there." The angel replied: "No, it's for you. God helps those who help themselves."

Of course, the moral of the story is not that it's all right to curse and there's nothing wrong with blaspheming. But anyone who sloughs off his responsibility onto God and does nothing but pray and make promises, without lifting a finger to solve his problems himself, does not understand what Christianity is all about.

God exists. Thank God He exists and can intervene in

Creation whenever He pleases. But here is a teaching that is basic to Christianity and an opening statement capable of nourishing the development mystique: God created man in His own image. God trusts man to master nature and finish the work of Creation.

Our liturgy must give a fuller and more Biblical meaning to solemnities such as the Lenten and other fasts. Instead of showing God as the Lord of the winds and waters, the seeds, plants, and harvests, let us show the Creator Who from His overflowing heart, without fear of shadows, without jealousy unworthy of God, gave man ample powers over the waters and winds, power over all Creation.

The liturgy must give fuller and more Biblical meaning to the worship of the saints. Instead of being pictured as magical beings, let them appear to our eyes as brothers who faced difficulties as great as our own and conquered them.

This was true of the Holy Family itself. Our Lady was already the Mother of God when, instead of losing herself in her own happiness, she went to her cousin St. Elizabeth's house to do whatever was needful. St. Joseph was a carpenter and lived by the sweat of his brow. And Christ Himself, the Son of God become man to save us, Christ doubtless had calluses on His hands.

The liturgy must help us to understand the true meaning of the eucharistic lesson: how can one who partakes of the bread of Love be selfish? How can one who feeds on God Himself be petty and think only of himself? But then, how can one who feeds on God Himself have anything to fear?

A *nordestino* told a friend: "*Compadre,* somebody, I don't know who, said that somewhere, I don't rightly know where, somebody's a-selling beans I don't know for how much."

He could hardly be much vaguer than that: he doesn't know who said it, doesn't know where, or who's doing the selling, or at what price. Until we stop idle speculation and vague hopes, until we create an ethic of work, effort, sacrifice, seeking, we will not be ready in our minds for development. The Bible lays a foundation for such a work ethic in Our Father's order to "cultivate our garden," that is, to cultivate the earth.

When the garden is Amazônia, everything about it is so gigantic that one hardly knows where to begin. But the vastness of the undertaking should be a challenge, not an excuse.

I once spoke in Goiânia before groups of professors and students from various departments of the Federal and Catholic Universities. I unrolled a map of Goiás for them to see. I reminded them that their state might be considered as part of the Middle West, since it joins Mato Grosso, or in relation to the Northeast, since it abuts on that region from Bahia to Maranhão.

But the greatest responsibility of the state of Goiás comes of its sharing a border with Amazônia: Goiás' North is one of the roads into Amazônia.

With those groups of university students and professors we sketched a working plan for Amazônia, beginning with a study of Amazonian Goiás, with camping trips and expeditions which would give the Amazonians of Goiás a deeper awareness of the urgent necessity of taming Amazônia for the service of man.

Why should not similar appeals be made in Manaus and Belém, to the university students and professors who should be living examples of the ethic of cultivating the earth?

And now a third episode, leading up to a third aspect of the development mystique: the destruction of Hiroshima and Nagasaki.

On the day the first atomic bomb was dropped, at the exact moment when the world felt a thrill of horror, someone remarked: "Hiroshima has suffered for us. The day will come when the enormous power of the atom, which we have had a glimpse of today, will be used for peaceful ends and for the good of humanity."

Those words came from a man eighty years old, an old man to whom the authentic vision of Christ assured a perennial youth. Those who stand aghast at the sudden upflarings of human intelligence do not understand Christianity. There are those who are appalled at seeing man leap over walls that once enclosed dominions seen as belonging exclusively to God. There are those who tremble at man's self-intoxication, at his assumption that he no longer has any need of God but is ready to take His place and do all of the things that only God has done before.

Christianity has an answer for the human thirst to become God. The Son of God became man to bring us Grace, which is participation in the Divine Nature itself.

Is it any wonder, then, that man created in God's image; man, made divine by Grace, should perform prodigies that our grandfathers thought forever beyond man's reach?

When Brazil, turning a deaf ear to the egoism of the superpowers, demands the right to the peaceful use of atomic energy, it must have in mind regions like Amazônia.

How can we conquer Amazônia without the atom to help us drag rivers from their beds, fill in swamps, make oil burst out of the ground, slash through virgin jungle, act as a demiurge? Now is the time for the development ethic to spur us on, recalling from the Bible that God made man a little lower than the angels, and, in the words of St. Paul, that we are as gods.

There is a story going around which started here in Recife and has spread throughout Brazil: that foreigners are distributing contraceptive pills to depopulate Amazônia altogether and make it easier to take it over eventually.

One never knows whether or not there is any truth to such tales, which spread like fire in a haystack; but true or false, this one raises one of the gravest problems of underdevelopment: the population explosion. The experts have found that the rate of economic growth in the developing countries is nullified by the rate of population growth. This being the case, there are those who believe in all seriousness that the Pill is the answer.

How is the development ethic to cope with population growth?

Let us begin by noting the inanity of the Pill. The Pill as panacea is typical of the reasoning processes of the developed who know nothing of the psychology of the underdeveloped. For a "developed" couple, a child is an expense long before he is born; as early, even, as prenuptial examination. When it looks as if the child is on the way, there in another examination to verify pregnancy; the pregnant woman is cared for by gynecologists; there are special treatments to forestall varicose veins and other ailments stemming from pregnancy. The birth takes place in a clinic. Then it's the pediatrician's turn. And special food. And toys. And tiny garments. And then it's time for nursery school, and then kindergarten. And private school, more expensive every year. And university. For a developed couple, a child weighs heavily on the family budget.

For the underdeveloped, a child weighs much less. He just means finding room for one more, that's all. No, there can't be any prenuptial examination; no pregnancy test, no gynecologist in attendance, no health clinic, no pediatrician; no proper food, nor toys, nor tiny garments; no nursery school, nor kindergarten, nor high school, nor university . . . just whatever odds and ends the family can spare.

For the underdeveloped, a son begins to work early and works until he marries. After he is married, the new daughter-in-law means another pair of hands to wield a hoe.

In the undeveloped Northeast, the birth of a child is greeted with fireworks. The least you can do for a new baby is set off a rocket.

Within the development ethic, while keeping our eyes open to the importance of responsible procreation, let us help teach parents to set a high value on every child.

Room must be made for human beings. Shaking Amazônia out of its lethargy, turning it upside down, developing it, makes no sense unless it is done for the benefit of man. Not just for the benefit of a few privileged men. Any and every child of man has been in our Father's thoughts for all of eternity; was redeemed by the blood of God's Son; is accompanied and protected by the Holy Spirit. Any and every son of man has the right to call God his Father.

When a king's son makes a visit of state, a whole complicated protocol is followed to honor the prince. Can too much honor be paid to the dignity of one who is not merely a king's son, but a son of God?

One day when I saw the neighbors in a poor and humble community helping one another, I could not hide my joy at seeing this manifestation of brotherly spirit. One of the men remarked in his colloquial speech: "That's the way it has to be, because believe you me, nobody likes us but us."

This phrase comes to mind when I think of the urgent need, not only for the North and the Northeast to love one another like brothers and help complete and complement one another, but for the same thing to happen in Brazil as a whole, and all over Latin America.

The development mystique can draw enormous benefit from the circumstance that Providence has placed the Northeast and Amazônia side by side; that it has reserved to the same Christian religion and almost identical languages the task of unifying not only Brazil, but our entire continent. It cannot be repeated too often that this fraternal union will never be a source of hate and radical violence toward other continents or other nations.

The development ethic will lead us by gradual stages toward universal solidarity: brotherhood between the North and Northeast; national integration; continental integration; Third World; Humanity.

All of this may sound like empty fantasy, castles in the air. Our wondering eyes see two spirals going in opposite directions: the spiral of underdevelopment, descending at ever-increasing speed through vicious circles of cumulative negative conditions; and the spiral of development, which spins higher and higher through virtuous circles and cumulative positive conditions.

Is it really possible to move from one spiral to the other? Is it possible to break out of underdevelopment without paying a price in hatred? And is it not here that the definitive failure of Christianity as a development ethic lies?

Let no one be deceived as to the nature of Christ. There is no doubt that He came to bring peace to men. But not the peace of stagnant swamps, not peace based on injustice, not a peace that is the opposite of development. In such cases, Christ Himself proclaimed that He had come to bring strife and a sword.

Alas for those with no heart for the struggle, the satiated, those who have lost their hunger and thirst for justice. Alas for those who love their own lives and do not know how to lose them. Alas for those who cling to their reputations, honor, and convenience. Christ crowned the beatitudes by naming as most blessed among the blessed those who suffer persecution for the sake of justice.

The bishops of Brazil have called more loudly than anyone for reforms in society, agrarian reform in particular.

There are examples of bishops who are making successful attempts at encouraging the human and Christian advancement of families who live on diocesan lands in subhuman conditions.

Let us nonetheless find the courage to face an unpleasant situation from which there is no use trying to run away: it is still the exception rather than the rule for diocesan lands to be used in wholehearted effort to humanize the wretched folk who vegetate in areas belonging to the Church.

What is it that so frequently prevents Brazilian bishops, including the Bishop of Olinda and Recife, from illustrating our ringing calls for agrarian reform by our own example?

Two great difficulties stand in our way:

• We know it is not enough to tell a tenant farmer that the land belongs to him for him to be suddenly transformed into the human being we dream of his becoming. There must be a simultaneous, complementary offering of technical assistance, financial assistance, social assistance, and spiritual assistance for that to happen.

• We know, too, that if we simply announce to the farmer that he is now the owner of the land he lives on, we are affording a golden opportunity for unscrupulous confidence men to buy the new owner's land and shack for a trifle and leave him worse off than he was before.

Our lack of resources to effect a genuine program of human advancement on lands belonging to the diocese is perpetuating this untenable situation, one in which we suffer every disadvantage and not a single real advantage.

How long will we let this equivocal situation drag on? The National Bishops Conference of Brazil has announced its decision to carry out a broad survey of diocesan holdings. It seems impossible to postpone this embarrassing question any longer, at least in the Northeast, for it undermines our moral position when we demand what we must in the way of agrarian reform. We will offer specific, feasible suggestions in this matter. But first we have other faults to confess.

It should be of grave concern to us that after investigating the state of land reform in seven Latin-American countries, including Brazil, an official organ like the Inter-American Agricultural Development Committee reached the conclusion that agrarian reform *is not working;* that it is limited to the promulgation of fine-sounding laws and the creation of bureaus whose mission is that of making radical changes in agrarian structure. No one has the right so to mock one of the essential hopes of the masses.

As an example, take what is occurring in the sugar-cane fields of the Northeast. Five federal bureaus—SUDENE, the Bank of Brazil, the Institute of Sugar and Alcohol, the Brazilian Institute of Agrarian Reform, and the National Institute of Agrarian Development—signed an agreement and founded GERAN, the Northeast Agro-Industrial Executive Group. Nothing could be finer in theory: GERAN undertook to provide the technical resources to modernize the sugar mills, with the proviso that once they were producing more sugar on less land, they would willingly surrender the land they no longer needed. On this land, the Institutes of Agrarian Reform and Agrarian Development were to initiate genuine agrarian reform, a program of real human advancement, for they would not limit themselves to giving each worker a piece of land, but would give him land plus technical, financial, and social assistance.

Let us hope that GERAN will not drag its feet and remain nothing but an acronym.

It is encouraging to note that SUDENE, the official entity responsible for the economic development of the whole Northeast, has been obliged for economic reasons to set up a Human Resources Department, and under it a Community Action Division. It is encouraging, too, to read what SUDENE understands by Community Action:

It is the social process through which a human group in a determined area, interrelated through socioeconomic and cultural ties, consciously promotes change, either spontaneous or induced, in order to facilitate and accelerate the emergence of economic and psychosocial conditions conducive to a continuing development.

It is just as encouraging to learn, apropos of social change, that for SUDENE:

Development also means breaking away from outmoded economic, psychosocial, and mental patterns which are still strong enough to determine a way of life whose by-products are misery and a subhuman existence.

Experience has taught us that the treatment accorded those who act in the field of social work varies completely according to whether one stops at social welfare or feels the necessity to go beyond it and struggle for the human advancement of men who are not yet men.

If you stop with social welfare, distributing food, clothes, and medicine or even encouraging artisanry, cooperatives, and simple literacy, you'll be accorded consideration and esteem.

But the day you realize that all this is not enough and that it is necessary to fight for the right of your brothers dragged down by misery to live as human beings, you will fall under suspicion and be looked on as a subversive, a pawn of the Communists.

We have even witnessed the absurdity of seeing one of the most beautiful expressions of the democratic vocabulary— *conscientização*—condemned as a word that, if not actually red, was certainly tinged with pink. What could be more democratic than awakening a numbed consciousness, which implies goading a man's intelligence and encouraging his sense of freedom, two of the highest gifts bestowed on man by God?

How long will the experts in community action have to go on doing their work under a cloud of suspicion, fearful not so much for themselves (as a rule, the higher up you are, the freer you are of specific constraints), but of what will assuredly happen to the humble folk whose consciousness is being aroused?

And nothing is more prejudicial, nothing causes more tragic delay, nothing hinders the sacred and pressing work of *conscientização* so much as tearing down a man's shack and expelling him from the land for the ugly crime of joining a union, demanding the rights the law says he has, such as minimum wages, job security, pensions, and retirement benefits, and even attending a radiophonic school. Nothing so retards the democratic process, nothing so deeply disturbs community development, as persecuting a man whose subversive activity lay in beginning to open his eyes to his own rights, without forgetting his obligations. What a difficult task it is to reorganize groups of neighbors—that fertile seedbed of human advancement and community action—once they have been terrorized by finding themselves harassed for their democratic, human, Christian initiative. Hounded and persecuted as Communists!

I am not propounding a hypothetical case, but describing events that happened only yesterday, events which I hope will never again be repeated in Brazil.

What, specifically, can be done to ensure for the experts in community development not only peace of mind but the indispensable moral influence over the people among whom they work?

Experiments are being attempted here by those universities which are trying to break out of their cocoon of alienation to become a part of the real world around them. This is a first step toward national integration in the sense of a joint effort to bring every part of our territory and every group in our population into the mainstream of national life. The universities of the Northeast and the North understand more and more plainly the burden of responsibility they bear because they are located in areas where the regime is one of internal colonialism and the situation of two-thirds of the population is subhuman. Wouldn't it be appropriate for SUDENE and SUDAM, the Superintendency for Amazonian Development, to arrange a meeting between universities in the North and the Northeast, to evaluate and encourage experiments like the community development program sponsored by the Regional University Council of Bahia and the Northeast? Of course the aim would be to serve, to exchange experiences, to stimulate university reform by action, with the enormous added advantage of giving moral support to community action.

We have no right to work unilaterally. We must not lose our cool objectivity and turn to radical actions which would be a disaster for community development.

Why not adopt a new frame of reference? Why not try, perhaps in a more skillful, surer, more scientific way, to do what each of us individually has already tried to do without success: begin a meaningful dialogue with business executives, particularly those operating in critical areas?

The businessmen feel that they are not being heard. As they see it, their problems are not understood and are not fairly expressed. When they hear talk of internal colonialism—meaning that of Brazilians whose wealth is based on the oppression of other Brazilians—it exasperates them, and although admitting that the term may accurately describe certain areas, maintain that it is simply not valid for all.

They complain of misunderstanding, neglect, and extortion on the part of the state and federal governments; of a Church growing more leftist, violent, and radical day by day; of workers growing less and less friendly and more and more demanding and radical. They have problems to face; difficulties they cannot solve by themselves; good will which needs only trust, understanding, and support in order to become meaningful. Who has given us the right to draw the line? In the name of what human, Christian principles are we called upon to judge any tentative rapprochement as useless and counterproductive? Who gives us the authority to condemn these men and pray for fire and sulfur to descend on their heads?

The Brazilian Institute of Agrarian Reform, with the help of SUDENE and SUDAM, should study the feasibility of arranging meetings with entrepreneurs in the North and Northeast, perhaps following some such general guidelines as these:

- Single out entrepreneurs by groups, since the problems are different for sugar-mill owners, rubber tappers, cattle raisers, cotton and sisal planters, and businessmen who are starting new industries, to mention only a few.
- Find a way to make the transition from meetings among business owners to meetings between owners and workers.

Of course, authentic representation is just as important in the case of the workers as it is for the owners. It would be an inadmissible perversion of the spirit of such meetings to fear the presence and actions of real labor leaders and instead entrust the job of speaking for the workers to political stooges. The groundwork for the meetings should be laid carefully by surveying the areas to be discussed and inviting experts in those specific fields of study to be present.

8

The Redemption of the Northeast

The eyes of Brazil and of all the world are on the Northeast. Have you noticed that the Northeast has become a national theme and a cynosure of international interest? However, the image portrayed is nearly always distorted, both in this country and abroad.

The Northeast is a cliché now, a slogan. But the cliché must be made objective; the slogan must be corrected.

Professional misery is unacceptable to the Northeast, and it cannot and should not tolerate being looked upon as the powder keg of Latin America.

Let us rally around the decision to make the Northeast anticipate the Brazil of tomorrow and foreshadow a new Latin America and a new Third World.

Let us unite, for authentic development cannot be the work of one group or one class. Either the whole region and every group in it will develop, or we will be left with a distorted mimicry of development.

This is why I cannot be satisfied with begging bosses and workers, rich and poor, left and right, believers and nonbelievers, merely to agree to a truce. What is needed is dialogue, broad, confident, and ever-growing. It is a grave sin in the eyes of God and of history to refuse to rebuild the world.

Let us accelerate our work of development without delay, accepting it as an evangelizing Christian mission. It will profit us nothing to venerate beautiful images of Christ, nor even to stop before a poor man and recognize in him the disfigured face of Our Savior, if we do not see Christ in the human being waiting to be saved from underdevelopment.

Strange as it may seem to some, I say to you that in the Northeast Christ's name is Zé, Antônio, Severino. . . . *Ecce Homo:* here is Christ, behold the Man! He is the man—in need of justice, deserving justice, with a right to justice.

If we are to keep the oppressed from doing sterile and destructive violence, we must go beyond the apparent harmony that masks the absence of real dialogue.

Instead of being indignant when he sees his workers banding together for mutual support, their employer should be honest and truthful enough to admit that only in very exceptional cases will a worker be heard and heeded without the support of his fellows. But workers' associations are morally enfeebled when they go beyond just limits. Undue use of force by the bosses must not be traded for undue use of force by the workers. Dialogue implies mutual respect and a modicum of trust and good will.

Let us pray to Christ, the true Priest whom the human priest represents, to celebrate the holy sacrifice of the Mass for the world, especially for Brazil, and particularly for the Northeast.

And may this region, which has won through crushing misfortune and faltering hopes to begin the rise toward development, show Brazil an example of dynamic peace based on justice, of truth in charity, of dialogue and fraternal understanding, above the divisions that are dragging this country to the brink of civil war and chaos. May the Northeast lead Brazil in rapid recuperation from the political crisis through which we have just passed. Without jeopardizing national security or relaxing the alert against Communism, let us not brand as Communists those who simply hunger and thirst for social justice and for the development of their country.

May the Northeast help keep Brazil from defrauding the hopes of its people. Let us prove that democracy is capable of eradicating our evils.

And may we, the spiritual leaders of the Northeast, ever bear in mind that God has not entrusted disembodied souls to our keeping, but human creatures with both bodies and souls. As long as only a few leaders carry on the battle for development—not by usurping the tasks of the experts but by bearing Christian witness to their mission and encouraging their efforts in behalf of human advancement—as long as only a few of us join the other vital forces in the Northeast, those few will be easily marked down by the Communists, among others. In a region like ours, for the Communists "the worse things are, the better" —an ideal culture for the fermentation of despair.

If all of us, while mindful of eternal life, demand human conditions for human beings on earth; if all of us make up our minds to go beyond mere aid and carry out human and social advancement, then it will soon become clear that the hour of change has struck.

The President of the Republic has stated many times that the end and aim of his government is man. The hour has struck when the federal government must help the Northeast escape from the paradox of increasing economic growth and decreasing human growth.

The vital forces of the Northeast are ready to help SUDENE in a mighty effort to make of the Fourth Guiding Plan, which covers the crucial 1968–70 triennial, a solution to the problems of the Northeast of today.

But this implies brave, firm measures of national and international policy:

• On the national plane, instead of counterposing other regional plans to ours, the central government should throw its help and support to the Northeast.

• It is on the continental plane that the key to the problem of national underdevelopment may be found. Authentic dialogue between a very rich and powerful country and a very poor and helpless country is practically an impossibility. No

Latin-American country is in a position to stand up to the blocs whose intention it is to divide the world between them. For the sake of universal dialogue, it is urgently necessary that our continent unite and strengthen itself. If this is to be accomplished, it would seem to be of prime importance for the Latin-American Common Market to avoid being dashed to pieces on either of two perilous reefs: that of becoming someone else's satellite and that of allowing to arise on our continent, by the actions of the larger countries like Brazil, Argentina, and Chile, the sort of imperialistic evils practiced on smaller neighbors which so embitter us when practiced on ourselves.

• Brazil has recently taken some important steps on the international plane. Instead of being tied to the anachronism of reasoning in terms of East and West (that is, in terms of Communism and anti-Communism), it has become realistic enough to see the world in terms of North and South; that is, in terms of development and underdevelopment.

Whoever visits the First Fair of Commerce and Industry of the Northeast, in Recife, can take the exact measure of the rising Northeast. Benefiting from tax incentives designed to promote this area's development, industry is multiplying at an encouraging rate. And the *nordestino*'s capacity for improvisation is truly amazing. Foreign or Southern technicians are brought in only when strictly necessary. The rest of the staff is recruited right here. The first thing to catch our admiration is the construction of the factories themselves, for they are no ordinary buildings. Almost all of the new industries require complicated, specialized installations. But the really wonderful part is to see practically illiterate, untrained *nordestinos* working with petroleum, assembling automobiles, fitting bodies for trucks and cars, putting batteries together, plunging into the mysteries of electronics and petrochemistry, rigging bases for space rockets, laying the foundations of heavy industry. The *nordestino* brain sparkles with intelligence. If you want to keep your technique a secret, don't put anything together or take it apart where we can watch you do it; don't repeat any complex operation more than twice.

Just think what our men will be able to do tomorrow, if today, without any training, they can learn the most difficult, demanding techniques in the wink of an eye! Just think what our men will do tomorrow, if even today, sick, undernourished, wretched as they are, they have grit enough to make well-nourished supermen take off their hats to them!

There was a time when the basic problem of the Northeast was thought to be water. Dams sprang up everywhere, but served only a privileged minority because the government had not had the foresight and political courage to make them serve the common good.

Let us have the basic network of highways, and the over-hauling of our ports, with their logical and indispensable warehouses; let the Northeast be included in the national tele-communications system; let there be power; let there be irriga-tion; give us aid for the economy of products vital to the Northeast; let our basic goods and seeds be commercialized; let there be rural credit facilities, effective minimum-price guarantees for agricultural products, and an industry of phos-phate fertilizers; let mineral prospecting and mining be modern-ized; let us search for potassium; let Petrobras drill for oil. But above everything, let effective measures be taken to ensure that all this effort is made, not for the benefit of a few, but to promote the development of the whole Northeast and of every *nor-destino*.

People with no understanding of technical problems tend to be dismayed when they hear so much talk of agrarian reform and then see nothing being done about it as time passes. Or-ganizations are created with fanfare and fancy names. One was called SUPRA, but it did not succeed in spite of its name. Then IBRA (the Brazilian Institute of Agrarian Reform) and INDA (the National Institute of Agrarian Development) came into the limelight. But suddenly, as if they were being demoted or needed more control in order to act a little more slowly, they returned to the Ministry of Agriculture whence they had come.

Of course the government has the right to undertake whatever administrative reforms it thinks necessary. With no equivocal or carping intention, I am simply speaking for those who cannot make themselves heard. It does not matter which organization carries out reform. It is not necessary to wait for an ideal law to appear. But let there be *some* law, and let it come soon, and let it be enforced.

Once in the sugar-cane zone of our Northeast, we came as close as we have ever come to the reforms for which we long.

Five official organizations (the Bank of Brazil, SUDENE, the Institute of Sugar and Alcohol, IBRA, and INDA) signed an agreement and GERAN (Agro-Industrial Executive Group of the Northeast) was born. The plan was ideal: GERAN would undertake to furnish new equipment for the sugar mills, with the guarantee that they would produce three or four times as much sugar as they do now. In return, land that was no longer in use would revert to GERAN and become the starting point for the genuine human advancement of the farm workers who are still chained to a subhuman life. Together with their piece of land, they would receive technical, financial, and social assistance.

But just when we thought that reform was beginning at last, GERAN's name was changed to Special Group instead of Executive Group. The initials remained the same, but my long-suffering people, who hadn't much hope to lose, lost hope.

It's a curious thing that the portion of a law affecting the sugar-cane zone that benefits the owners is put into effect on the spot, while the part that benefits the workers takes time, and usually an exceedingly long time.

Back in President Vargas' time, Law by Decree No. 6969, signed October 19, 1944, guaranteed every sugar-cane worker in the Northeast five acres of land for subsistence farming. More than twenty years later the decree was still waiting to be put into effect when it was renewed and brought up to date by a new Law by Decree, No. 57020, dated October 11, 1965, and signed by President Castelo Branco. Let us hope that it doesn't take so long to be enforced this time. Speaking directly to farm workers in Cabo, President Costa e Silva assured them that the five-acre law will be put into effect. The workers have already warned the President that they have their doubts about a big windfall they've been promised: there's talk of three hundred acres instead of five.

It is easy to laugh at the five-acre solution. It is easy to heap ridicule on this agrarian mini-reform. The workers are asking for five acres as an emergency solution, which will have the enormous merit of rescuing them from starvation and proletarianization while testing their courage and love of the land with a view to future selection for a genuine agrarian reform. What good does it do to adduce theoretical reasons for not giving them five acres, when triumphant experiments have already been carried out on sugar plantation land which was given to the workers in lieu of wages?

Only love can build. Hate and violence only destroy. What valid, democratic solution remains then to an underdeveloped country attempting to open the eyes of the elite to the advisability of accepting *conscientização,* the preparation of a people for development, and the indispensable reform of medieval structures?

I am thinking specifically of a broad experiment embracing the whole of the Brazilian Northeast, along the lines of the admirable movement for racial integration led in the United States by the Reverend Martin Luther King.

I used to think, when I was a child, that Christ might have been exaggerating when He warned about the dangers of wealth. Today I know better. I know how very hard it is to be rich and still keep the milk of human kindness. Money has a dangerous way of putting scales on one's eyes, a dangerous way of freezing people's hands, eyes, lips, and hearts. That is the source of my conviction that it is both democratic and Christian to bolster human frailty with a balanced, firm, and just moral pressure based on nonviolent action.

Development in the Northeast cannot afford to fail. Failure here would have tragic repercussions, crushing the hopes of our people and affecting all the rest of our country with repercussions, too—let us not deceive ourselves on this point—in Latin America and the whole of the Third World.

We have the right and the duty to sound all the warnings we deem necessary; to make any accusations that should in good conscience be made; to encourage, question, propose, deplore, rejoice, question men, and speak to God. Our right to do this is rooted precisely in the conviction that what is at stake is the destiny of our people, our own flesh and blood. No one has any monopoly on development: either it becomes everybody's job or it will never be anything but a blaze of fireworks, a cupola without a base.

Neither the government, nor the corps of technical experts, nor the owners of business firms, nor anyone else has the right to call the balance sheet we are here trying to draw up together "undue interference." On the contrary: even if the balance sheet includes some mistakes, as is only natural, it is born of so much love, of such a strong desire to get it right, that it deserves to be greeted with respect and pored over with joy; for it bears witness to our determination not to admit the least error when it comes to setting up the launching platform for the development of the whole man and of all men in this part of the world that God has given us.

It is fairly well known in the developed world that one of the fundamental preconditions for development is a people prepared to participate in it. The difficult thing for the developed world to comprehend is that there is a task to be done even before the people are prepared for development, and that is to help the masses living in subhuman conditions to become a people.

My impressions of our own situation as regards this primary stage can be summed up as follows:

• Young people are right when they protest, with their natural exuberance, against the decided alienation that still prevails in the universities of the Northeast. While it is true that some of them show promising signs of wanting to immerse themselves in regional problems, there are other universities that might as well be in São Paulo, Madrid, or London, on the moon instead of on earth, and of which it would be charitable to say that instead of living in the beginning of the twenty-first century they are living, to give them every benefit of the doubt, in the nineteenth.

• Working here for national integration inevitably means pointing an accusing finger at internal colonialism, the system through which some Brazilians base their wealth on the misery of other Brazilians kept in a subhuman state. To rail against this accusation and call it subversive is as absurd and ridiculous as it was absurd and ridiculous to oppose the abolition of slavery in 1885 or 1886.

• Without denying the dedication of those who are working to make our people literate, let us have the wit to see clearly that literacy alone is not enough to enable men to overcome the heritage of misery and the deep marks it leaves: marks of subservience stemming from utter, abject dependence on a *patrón* or a landlord, marks of pessimism bordering on fatalism, marks of an almost incurable inner despair.

• If we are working for national integration here, if we are struggling to pull millions of *nordestinos* into the mainstream of national life, then all the vital forces of this region, particularly those above suspicion such as religion and the universities, must lend their moral support to the indispensable, unpostponable work of awakening our masses through *conscientização*, that beautiful, oft-misunderstood expression by which is meant the effort to awaken our people's initiative, foster qualities of leadership, teach them how to work as a team and not to wait for everything to come from the government, to acknowledge their own obligations, but equally to know their rights and to demand them.

Our moral support must extend as far as the no less urgent and no less indispensable work of politicization in the beautiful, democratic, Christian sense of that word as interest and participation in public life, in the problems of one's neighborhood and one's region, in community action.

If we are not to remain theoretical, our balance sheet must go on to protest situations that are crying for immediate action from the public authorities:

• It is nothing less than a scandal that in spite of SUDENE, IAA, IBRA, INDA, and GERAN, the agricultural and industrial workers of the Northeast are still hungry and the situation is growing worse. We will have sinned by omission if we show ourselves incapable of finding adequate peaceful solutions to a problem that has already been talked to death.

• It has been said that it was not the floods that created the misery; it was already there. All the floods did was expose it in all its stark brutality.

Now I have, concerning the flood of 1966, one admirable fact to relate and two accusations to make: one serious, the other very grave indeed.

The admirable fact is that our people worked shoulder to shoulder with the government in the reconstruction campaign. The government spent 700,000 New Cruzeiros in construction materials, enough to repair, rebuild, or partially improve 6,767 of the 16,208 houses that were damaged. The people of the Northeast spent 151,000 New Cruzeiros on building materials. And of paramount importance is the fact that since the flood victims themselves provided all of the labor (this in itself was an experiment in politicization and self-awareness), since labor costs ordinarily represent 30 percent of the total cost of construction, we can and should point out that the people's contribution to this cooperative effort was actually 30 percent of the

850,000 New Cruzeiros budgeted for the project: that is, 255,000 New Cruzeiros.

The serious accusation is that SUDENE is not getting the funds it requested for repairing or rebuilding the remaining 9,441 houses still awaiting materials. Surely our long-suffering people, who showed such an extraordinary spirit of cooperation, deserve better of the government than to have the work stop when it is only half finished. It would indeed be a serious misfortune to dissipate the effect of this first large-scale attempt of the government and the people to work together.

The very grave accusation I make in good conscience: it is my duty as a pastor, as an eyewitness to the distress of our people, to do so, and I draw it to the special attention of the engineers of Pernambuco: a year has come and gone, and emergency repairs have been made; but unless I am much mistaken, we are right back where we started insofar as getting at the root of the trouble, which means taming the Capiberibe and Beberibe rivers. As for the clearing of the canals, when will the work begin in earnest? We do not wish to incriminate anyone: each administrator, and perhaps he and no one else, knows the problems he has to face. But let me leave you with this distressing thought: what will become of Recife if we have another flood like the flood of 1966?

Our balance sheet so far has been confined to purely technical areas. But now that we are entering the domain of development in the true sense of the word, I will make a quick outline of observations about items I consider essential. Here is one of the first:

1. Brazil urgently needs to invest much more in research than she is doing now. And just as urgently, she needs to get more good out of what research has already been done by coordinating data and duly profiting from whatever findings are valid. Is there anyone who is ignorant of the fact that one of the most serious and the most rapidly widening gaps between the

developed and the underdeveloped worlds is that pertaining to advanced technology?

We can't go on bleeding ourselves white paying royalties. We must develop our own national know-how, made in Brazil, made in Recife. . . .

2. It is just as important and just as urgent to train middle-management technicians and community leaders as it is to have high-level experts. A thoroughgoing review of attitudes should be undertaken, and it ought to begin with the Church. Many of us are still too firmly convinced that humanism means Greco-Latin humanism. What made us humanists, we thought, was Latin and Greek, and Greek and Latin literature. But we must open our minds once and for all to scientific humanism and help raise the status of technology in the eyes of everyone, at all levels and not only the highest.

3. A very positive note is struck by the fact that in our region development is not being thought of exclusively in economic terms. SUDENE, the official organization responsible for the economic development of the Northeast, has set an example by creating a Department of Human Resources and under it a Community Action Division. Development is a means to an end, and the end is man, marching toward God. Development merits an interdisciplinary effort. Development in the Northeast will not be complete until the poets, musicians, playwrights, philosophers, and theologians of development join the technicians.

4. We must try to make everyone who is responsible in some way for national planning understand that it is simple justice to treat those who are unequal in unequal ways: helping our undeveloped areas does no injury to the South and implies no discrimination within our federation of states.

The joy of seeing Southern industries investing more and more in the North, and creating new industries here, is marred only by the crisis through which Brazilian industry is passing. The doubt persists: is it true or false to say that domestic industry is hampered by credit restrictions, and very serious ones, while foreign industry is not?

While bearing no malice against any country whatever, we must make our leaders understand and take to heart what the people already sense: that when the amount of imported capital is compared with what is exported (that is, the money invested in Brazil compared with the sum that returns to the investors), and when aid received is compared with the losses which result from the low prices imposed on our raw materials, it is no exaggeration to say that our lifeblood is being drained away. Let us convince ourselves and then convince everyone else of this fact: the problem is not one of aid, but of justice on a global scale. Does such talk mean that we are anti-American? No, what we are really opposed to is misery, which is an insult to the Creator and Father. And incidentally, when will we learn to be as good Brazilians as Americans are good Americans? This does not mean shutting our doors on anyone; looking out for ourselves is not the same thing as becoming petty and nationalistic. But why should we try to be more American than the Americans? We want to see Brazil developed so as not to be a dead weight on the world, but, on the contrary, to create such a harmonious, unified civilization that our contribution to the world will be worthy of the gifts God gave our land and people.

Going back for a moment to the flood, let us recall an episode that will serve as a symbol and a warning.

The Catholic University of Pernambuco in Recife already knows how Severinos die, for several of its schools receive unidentified corpses for the students to dissect; and it is moving to see how respectfully agnostics and atheists attend the religious services that we Christians hold for our anonymous brothers, the abortive fruits of underdevelopment. During the flood the University Hospital was inundated by flood victims. Suddenly Severino's life came into the university: this less-than-life, this mean, lusterless, ineffective existence without health, without spirit, without life. It was a salutary lesson to the students at that university: it is up to them now to help other universities in the Northeast understand fully the warning from God that swept through their doors. They must help the universities of the Northeast lead the way in unfurling once and for all the banner of national integration.

THE AUTHOR

Dom Hélder Câmara was born in Fortaleza, Brazil, and ordained in 1931. He was consecrated as Bishop in 1952, and in 1955 named Auxiliary Archbishop of Rio de Janeiro, where he founded several organizations dedicated to working for the improvement of the economic and social conditions of the poor. For his work and his writings, Dom Hélder Câmara has received a Martin Luther King International Peace Prize and was nominated for the Nobel Peace Prize in 1970.

THE EDITOR

Ruth Nanda Anshen, philosopher and editor, plans and edits *World Perspectives, Religious Perspectives, Credo Perspectives, Perspectives in Humanism* and *The Science of Culture Series.* She also writes and lectures on the relationship of knowledge to the nature and meaning of man and existence.

71 72 73 10 9 8 7 6 5 4 3 2 1